Tintern Abbey is situated on the right bank of the River Wye at the southern end of the village of Tintern. It lies just off the A466 road, some 5 miles (8km) north of Chepstow and 11 miles (18km) south of Monmouth. It is just 6 miles (9.7km) north of Junction 22 on the M4. OS 1:50,000 sheet 162 (NGR SO534000).

Over this stile, and by this door I enter'd the abbey accompany'd by a boy who knew nothing, and by a very old man who had forgotten every thing; but I kept him with me, as his venerable grey beard, and locks, added dignity to my thoughts; and I fancied him the hermit of the place.

The way to enjoy Tintern Abbey properly, and at leisure, is to bring wines, cold meat, with corn for the horses; (bread, beer, cyder, and commonly salmon, may be had at the Beaufort Arms;) Spread your table in the ruins; and possibly a Welsh harper may be procured from Chepstow'

The Honourable John Byng, 1781, from *The Torrington Diaries*

Introduction:
Ruins in a Wooded Valley

'After passing a miserable row of cottages, and forcing our way through a crowd of importunate beggars, we stopped to examine the rich architecture of the west front; but the door being suddenly opened, the inside perspective of the church called forth an instantaneous burst of admiration, and filled me with delight, such as I scarcely ever before experienced on a similar occasion'
William Coxe,
An Historical Tour Through Monmouthshire
(London 1801)

This record of first impressions at Tintern Abbey by a late eighteenth-century traveller and historian echoes sentiments expressed time and again in contemporary accounts of these picturesque ruins. Coxe was far from alone in his admiration for Tintern. By his time the abbey had already become a busy tourist attraction where, as in some latter-day eastern bazaar, beggars and would-be guides touted visitors arriving by road or on pleasure cruises along the river from Monmouth. As early as the 1780s the majestic and then ivy-covered walls were caught up in a widespread 'romantic' vision of the past. Speculation concerning the origins and history of the ruins there may have been, but this was secondary to Tintern's rôle as a focus of sentimental observation, a subject for artists, and an inspiration to poets.

For the modern visitor, arriving some two centuries later, the ruins offer scarcely a less breath-taking sight. The beggars and ivy have long since disappeared, and alas boats are no longer used for excursions on the River Wye. But even so, sweeping around a road bend from Chepstow or Monmouth, one cannot fail to be impressed. The walls and arches rising from the narrow valley floor, surrounded by a tree-covered landscape of wild natural beauty, present a scene only rarely surpassed in these islands.

Today, although the details of the scene have changed slightly, many visitors will be asking much the same questions as the earliest tourists 200 years ago. Most people, for example, are likely to ask when and why Tintern was built, and to

A seal used by the abbots of Tintern sometime in the later twelfth to thirteenth centuries. A right hand emerges from a sleeve, and is holding a pastoral staff. The legend reads: +SIGILLVM ABBATIS DE TINTERNA (By permission of the National Museum of Wales).

'Tintern Abbey . . . Moonlight on the Wye' - A steel engraving published about 1830 (By courtesy of the National Library of Wales).

peculate upon the nature of the community which settled here, and the day to day life within the various parts of the building. Moreover, we may all wonder about the reasons for its remote setting in this wooded valley and, of course, we will ask why it was abandoned and allowed to fall into ruin.

This guide attempts to provide straightforward answers to these and other questions most frequently asked about Tintern. To this end, let us begin by considering why this remote spot in the Wye valley should have been chosen for such a magnificent building.

First Impressions

Travelling from Chepstow or Monmouth, the visitor may first pause and admire the beauty of the site. From the modern car park one gazes upon that same west front which greeted William Coxe.

The ruins which stand before you are the remains of Tintern Abbey, a medieval monastery established for monks of the Cistercian order by the Norman lord of Chepstow, Walter fitz Richard. The initial community of at least thirteen monks, from central France, settled here in 1131. From these infant beginnings, the abbey was to remain a centre of monastic life and prayer for 400 years. During that time it received the patronage of local lords, who bestowed upon it lands and privileges in various parts of Gwent, Gloucestershire and further afield. It was not until 1536, with the Dissolution of the Monasteries in the reign of Henry VIII, that monastic life ceased at Tintern.

The monks settling at Tintern, were the Cistercians. Such were the ideals and way of life of this order that they not only dictated the choice of site for the monastery, but also had an overriding influence upon the arrangement and development of the building complex.

3

The Cistercian Order

Monastic life was already centuries old when Tintern Abbey was founded. St Benedict had formulated his *Rule*, laying down the way of life for a Christian religious community, as far back as A.D. 540 at Monte Cassino in Italy. By the eighth

St Benedict, depicted in an early eleventh-century manuscript. Cistercian monastic life was based upon a strict interpretation of his Rule (Copyright: The British Library, Arundel Ms. 155, f. 133).

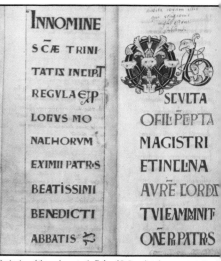

Beginning of the prologue to the Rule of St Benedict, from a manuscript written and illuminated about 1100 (Copyright: The British Library, Harley Ms. 5431, ff. 6b-7).

century this *Rule* had been widely adopted by monasteries throughout western Europe, which can thus be styled Benedictine. In England these were to receive serious setbacks during the Scandinavian invasions of the ninth century. However, from about 940 the Benedictines saw a great revival, and by the Norman Conquest they were well established in many parts of the country. In contrast, Wales had remained outside mainstream European monastic developments. From the sixth century onwards, it retained its own brand of Celtic monasticism, based on ideas initially introduced to its western shores by early missionary saints.

Almost inevitably, standards of discipline and devotion varied from one monastic house to another, but by the later eleventh century there was growing dissatisfaction with the régime of existing Benedictine abbeys. Gradually, there emerged a reforming spirit, a movement aimed at correcting abuses and introducing fresh ideals to the monastic life. It was from this impulse that the Cistercian order was born. It takes its name from Cîteaux (in Latin *Cistercium*), a monastery near Dijon in Burgundy (eastern France) where, in 1098, a group of pioneering monks settled to a new life of simplicity and asceticism.

The success of the order owed much to a strong constitutional framework, largely drawn up during the early abbacy (1109-34) at Cîteaux of an

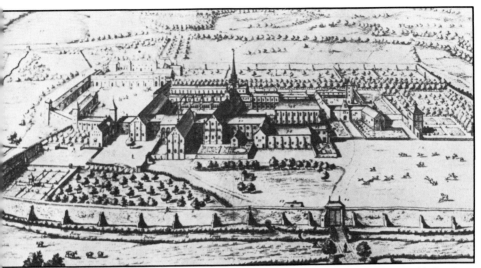

The foundation of Cîteaux in 1098 marked the beginning of the Cistercian order. Although badly damaged in the 'Wars of Religion' (1559-98), this etching of about 1670 by P. Brissart shows the abbey before its suppression in 1790.

nglishman, St Stephen Harding. This, with the riving force and personality of St Bernard of lairvaux, who joined the order in 1112, led to a ipid expansion of the Cistercians. Within forty years, by 1155, some 330 houses had been established in all parts of Europe.

Fearing the corrupting influence of riches on monastic zeal, the Cistercians placed a new emphasis on austerity and rejected all sources of luxury and wealth. Their constitution laid down strict rules for the location of new houses, and it is here that we find the explanation for Tintern's secluded position. Unlike those of the Benedictines, Cistercian abbeys were to be sited in isolation away from towns or villages, and 'remote from the habitations of men'. Their churches were to be plain and devoid of all ornament. They were to wear habits of undyed wool (hence they were known as the 'white monks'). There were strict rules of silence and diet, and their services were stripped of all the liturgical intricacies which had become attached to services at the older Benedictine monasteries. New abbeys could only be established under carefully laid down conditions. They were founded as colonies, or daughters, of existing houses and were to comprise of at least twelve monks with an abbot. Supervision was maintained throughout the order by a mutual system of visitation among mother and daughter houses, even if in different countries. In addition, an annual meeting, or General Chapter, was held at Cîteaux, at which all houses were to be represented.

isterican Abbeys in Europe

iteaux is shown, together with the French mother houses of the Cistercian bbeys in Wales (p.7). Tintern's mother, L'Aumône in Normandy, was founded 1121 (After J.M. Lewis and D.H. Williams 1976).

5

Choir Monks and Lay Brothers

During the formative years of the twelfth and thirteenth centuries, life within a Cistercian monastery could almost be seen as falling into two halves. This was, to a large extent, a result of the emphasis placed upon manual labour by the order. They were forbidden the customary 'feudal' sources of revenue such as tithes, manors, mills and rents, and therefore the intensive cultivation of agricultural land was as much an economic necessity, as it was an essential facet of the Cistercian monastic life. However, it was in the further stage of providing a labour supply to undertake this work, that the order proved so revolutionary.

Although the choir monks, those in full monastic orders, undertook some manual work, the greater part of the heavy agricultural labour was undertaken by lay brothers, or *conversi*. Recruited from amongst unlettered men, the latter made their contribution to religion by their labour. During the early Middle Ages they arrived at abbey gateways in large numbers, and often outnumbered the choir monks by two or three to one. Some lay brothers worked in the immediate vicinity of the abbey. Others travelled to work on outlying estates, usually within a day's journey of the home abbey, where lands had been acquired and organized into characteristic Cistercian farms, known as granges.

At the abbey, the lay brothers lived as part of the full community, though they were bound by less severe rules. None the less, as we shall see at Tintern, this division between choir monks and

Cistercian lay brothers depicted at work, in the form of capital letters (both C taken from a Cîteaux manuscript of the early twelfth century (By courtesy o. Bibliothèque Municipale, Dijon, Ms. 170, f. 59 and f. 75v).

conversi had powerful influences upon the architectural arrangement, of Cistercian monasteries.

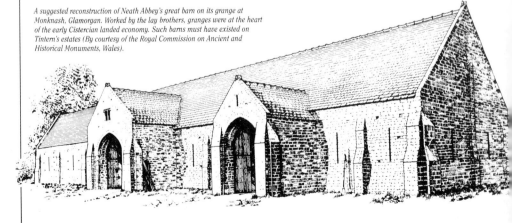

A suggested reconstruction of Neath Abbey's great barn on its grange at Monknash, Glamorgan. Worked by the lay brothers, granges were at the heart of the early Cistercian landed economy. Such barns must have existed on Tintern's estates (By courtesy of the Royal Commission on Ancient and Historical Monuments, Wales).

The Cistercians in England and Wales

The order was already well established in Western Europe when, in 1128, William Giffard, Bishop of Winchester, established the first Cistercian abbey on English soil. The site chosen was at Waverley (Surrey) and the house colonized from the Norman abbey of L'Aumône. As in

The remains of the dining hall at Waverley Abbey, the first Cistercian foundation in England (Copyright: National Monuments Record, England).

Europe, subsequent expansion was rapid, and by the end of King Stephen's reign (1154) some fifty new foundations had been added to the order. Yorkshire and the north became the cradle-land of Cistercian settlement in England, though Wales

An aerial view of Rievaulx Abbey, North Yorkshire. Founded in 1132, it became a premier Cistercian house, drawing brethren 'like bees to a hive', with up to 140 monks and almost 500 lay brothers in the twelfth century (Copyright: Cambridge University Collection).

also proved attractive to the white monks. In all, some 75 Cistercian monasteries were eventually established in England and Wales. Within the area of the modern Principality itself, apart from Tintern, there were a further twelve abbeys during

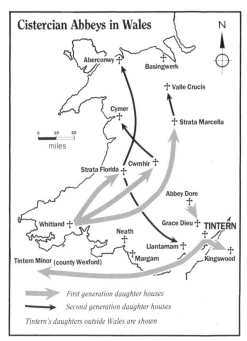

Cistercian Abbeys in Wales

N

Aberconwy
Basingwerk
Valle Crucis
Cymer
Strata Marcella
Strata Florida
Cwmhir
Abbey Dore
Whitland
Neath
Grace Dieu
TINTERN
Llantarnam
Kingswood
Tintern Minor (county Wexford)
Margam

0 10 20 miles

→ First generation daughter houses
→ Second generation daughter houses

Tintern's daughters outside Wales are shown

the Middle Ages. The course of their foundation and history, can virtually be seen in two distinct streams. On the one hand, those of the south and east such as Tintern itself, Margam (founded 1147) and Neath (becoming Cistercian 1147) were

The dormitory undercroft, probably the novices' lodging, at Neath Abbey, Glamorgan (By courtesy of the Royal Commission on Ancient and Historical Monuments, Wales).

founded by Anglo-Norman lords, and their subsequent fortunes were largely dependent upon later marcher lords. In contrast, the other stream lay in the heartland of Wales, with important foundations at Whitland (1140), Strata Florida (1164), Aberconwy (1186) and Valle Crucis (1201), all of which were patronized by native Welsh princes.

I Foundation to Dissolution: *A Brief History of Tintern Abbey*

The documentary evidence for the history of the abbey is far from extensive. Many Tintern manuscripts were probably stored at Raglan Castle, whose owners held much of the abbey's lands after the Dissolution, and were destroyed in the Civil War. Nevertheless, it is possible to present a broad outline of its growth from an infant plantation of the new Cistercian order, through to its position as probably the wealthiest monastery in Wales.

An aerial view of Tintern from the south-east. The magnificent abbey church i in the foreground, with the infirmary and abbot's complex in the sunlight to the right (Copyright: Cambridge University Collection).

At the Dissolution of the Monasteries, Tintern was granted to Henry, earl of Worcester, whose home was Raglan Castle. Many of the abbey's manuscripts were probably stored here, but were destroyed during the Civil War.

Tintern was never powerful or influential in the political sense, and its abbots played little part in national affairs, but the monks were important landowners and, as such, the abbey estates became a notable feature in the landscape of south-east Wales.

Tintern followed a trend similar to that of the Cistercians throughout England and Wales. During the early Middle Ages it was true to the ideals and constitution of the order. Buildings remained simple, and the monks proved rigorous in the cultivation of their own lands. This original simplicity and severity were, however, difficult to reconcile with the lavish gifts bestowed by rich patrons, and gradually buildings became more elaborate. What is more, the later medieval period was to witness widespread economic and social change. A declining lay brotherhood, coupled with the effects of the Black Death (1348-49), led to fundamental changes on abbey estates, which had to be leased out to tenants. By the early sixteenth century the abbot of Tintern had become little different from any secular landowner in the area.

Tintern Before the Abbey

At the foundation, the site chosen for the new abbey was reasonably isolated, though perhaps not entirely deserted. The lower Wye valley had been settled since prehistoric times. Bronze Age barrows, two small Iron Age hillforts, and evidence of Romano-British occupation are al known from near Tintern. Indeed, there was a small Roman settlement on the site of the later abbey.

In later tradition, a seventh-century Celtic King, Tewdric, is said to have become a hermit and lived 'amongst the rocks at Tintern'. In the following century, the Anglo-Saxon king, Offa, raised his dyke along the crest of the hills on the other side of the Wye.

Part of the initial endowment to the monks included lands at Porthcaseg, just south of the abbey, and it seems that these had been

intensively exploited before the foundation. Even so, there are no indications of a village or hamlet in the immediate vicinity of Tintern. Were this the case, the Cistercians were not beyond depopulating the settlement and pulling down the houses and even the church. They did just this in many parts of England and Wales.

Finally, we must not forget the town at Chepstow. Established by the Normans more than half a century before the foundation of Tintern, it lay just five miles (8km) downriver.

The Foundation and the Twelfth Century

Tintern was founded on May 9th 1131 by Walter fitz Richard de Clare, the Anglo-Norman lord of Chepstow and, as was customary with Cistercian abbeys, was dedicated to St Mary. It was only the second establishment of the order in the entire country, and was the very first in Wales. Like Waverley, three years before, it was colonized by monks from the Norman abbey of L'Aumône in the diocese of Chartres, itself a daughter house of Cîteaux. We know of continuing contacts between Tintern and the mother abbey until at least 1330. As to the size of the initial community, it is difficult to be sure, but it has been suggested that the endowments were intended for up to twenty monks and as many as fifty lay brothers.

An aerial view of Chepstow Castle from the south-east. From the founder onwards, the lords of Chepstow, including the Marshall family, Roger Bigod III, and William Herbert, all remained munificent benefactors of Tintern (Illustration by John Banbury).

The Early Acquisition of Lands

The new community depended upon landed possessions for its very existence. Where possible, gifts of land were organized into compact farms known as granges. Tintern eventually held up to twelve of these, of which Merthyrgeryn, Monkswood (or Estavarney), Moor, Rogerstone, Ruding, Secular Firmary and Trellech lay in Gwent, with Aluredeston, Ashwell, Brockweir, Modesgate and Woolaston across the Wye in Gloucestershire. The granges were not, however, the abbey's only estates and other land, including entire manors, was held in these areas, and even further afield. Much of this land was granted to the monastery before 1150, the founder himself giving various amounts at Porthcaseg, Penterry, Modesgate and Wilcrick. Thus, we must imagine the first generation of lay brothers vigorously preparing areas for cultivation, putting up grange buildings, and felling woods to extend the available plough land. Further properties were acquired throughout the Middle Ages, and the monks were constantly extending the size of existing estates through exchanges and small purchases.

Even before the close of the twelfth century, the drive to increase revenue led Tintern to ignore earlier Cistercian ideals and to acquire church tithes at Woolaston and Alvington, in Gloucestershire. The deposition of Abbot William in 1188, following a visitation from Cîteaux, may have been linked to this early breach of constitution. Even so, other churches were appropriated and tithes acquired in following centuries.

Daughter Houses

With youthful energy, Tintern grew rapidly, both in stature and in new recruits. In 1139 it was in a position to send out monks to a daughter house at Kingswood, Gloucestershire. By 1200 the abbey was able to establish a second daughter house at Tintern Minor, in county Wexford, Ireland. These were to remain its only colonies.

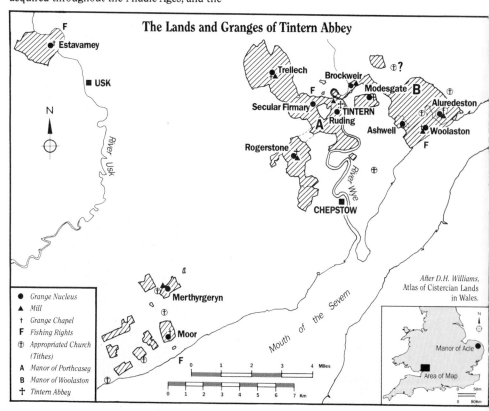

The Lands and Granges of Tintern Abbey

After D.H. Williams, Atlas of Cistercian Lands in Wales.

- ● Grange Nucleus
- ▲ Mill
- † Grange Chapel
- F Fishing Rights
- ⊕ Appropriated Church (Tithes)
- A Manor of Porthcaseg
- B Manor of Woolaston
- † Tintern Abbey

Arable land continued to be important, and from the middle of the century the monks were involved in draining the marshy coastal levels of Gwent, together with further woodland clearance. In 1282 the abbey was heavily fined for felling 200 acres (81ha) of forest at Woolaston without licence.

We gain some idea of the relative wealth Tintern had achieved by the close of the century from a taxation document known as the *Taxatio Ecclesiastica* of 1291. At the time, the abbey was farming well over 3,000 acres (1,214ha) of arable land, and its possessions were assessed at more than £145. This was small by the standards of many English houses, but sufficient to make Tintern the fifth wealthiest monastery in Wales. Margam, another Cistercian house, headed the list with an income of almost £256.

A late fourteenth-century gatehouse is all that survives of Tintern's daughter house at Kingswood, Gloucestershire, founded in 1139 (Copyright: National Monuments Record, England).

Effigy of a knight in chain armour, about 1240-50. It lay over the tomb of a benefactor in the abbey church, possibly one of the last Marshall heirs. The head is now lost, and the figure much worn. Taken from an illustration of about 1820 by David ap Thomas Powell (Illustration by C.A.P. Daly).

The Thirteenth and Early Fourteenth Centuries

By the beginning of the thirteenth century the lordship of Chepstow had passed by marriage to the powerful Marshall family, earls of Pembroke, which continued to support the monks at Tintern. Indeed, it was the enterprising William Marshall the elder who had founded the Irish daughter house. In 1223, William the younger confirmed earlier gifts and granted additional land at Monkswood (Estavarney). In 1224 he also gave lands at Rogerstone for a lamp in the abbey to be kept burning at the tomb of his mother, Isabel countess of Pembroke.

The burial of lay persons within Cistercian abbeys was not strictly permitted, but this was long overlooked at Tintern. From the founder onwards, noble patrons expected to be honourably interred; and, for the monks, lamps or a regular mass for the soul of the patron meant additional lands or income. The burial of the countess Isabel in 1220 was not the first such arrangement, nor was that of two of her sons in 1245 the last.

An extensive rebuilding programme begun in the early 1200s no doubt led the abbot and his officials to keep a close eye on estate profits.

A further indication of Tintern's status comes from the fact that between 1295 and 1305 the abbot, Ralph, was summoned to Parliament five times, possibly as much a reflection of Ralph's character as of his office. Twenty years later, in 1326, the only known royal visitor, Edward II, spent two nights at the abbey on his way from Gloucester to Chepstow.

King Edward II (1284-1327), who stayed at Tintern in 1326. From the alabaster tomb effigy in Gloucester Abbey, now the cathedral (By courtesy of the Conway Library, Courtauld Institute of Art).

Roger Bigod III: The 'Second Founder'

The most prominent patron of Tintern in the thirteenth and early fourteenth centuries was Roger Bigod III, earl of Norfolk (1270-1306), whose family had succeeded to Chepstow through

The arms of Roger Bigod III. On completion of the new thirteenth-century abbey church, these were eventually emblazoned in the great east window (see p.35).

marriage with a Marshall heiress. Much of the present fame of the abbey is a direct result of his interest in its affairs. Most significant of all was his rôle in supporting the rebuilding of the abbey church. Furthermore, in 1302 he granted the monks the Norfolk manor of Acle, their single most profitable asset, adding £50 to the total income of the house. He also went on to grant the abbey the manor of Alvington, Gloucestershire in exchange for other property, as well as the church of Halvergate in Norfolk.

The early fourteenth century saw Tintern at its zenith. Bigod, the 'second founder', had placed the house in a secure economic position, and this in a period fraught with difficulties for many religious houses. Apart from the church of Lydd in Kent, acquired sometime before 1351, Tintern made very few additions to its property after this time.

The Later Middle Ages

Evidence for the internal affairs of the abbey during the later Middle Ages remains fragmentary. Royal records do, nevertheless, tell us of a dispute concerning weirs on the River Wye in the early 1330s. They had been raised by the monastery for fishing purposes, but were restricting the passage of shipping. Henry earl of Lancaster, complained to the king that supplies were not reaching his town of Monmouth. The monks refused to cooperate and even assaulted officials sent to lower the weirs.

In 1348-49 the Black Death swept the country and, although we have no direct evidence for its impact on Tintern, the effects are clear. It became almost impossible to attract new recruits for the lay brotherhood. Widespread changes in the economy, with feudal service giving way to a system based on wages, were increased by labour shortages following the plague. At the grange of Merthyrgeryn in 1387-88 most of the area formerly worked by lay brothers had been leased out to tenants. The general situation at Tintern is perhaps best summed up by the changing rôle of the abbey cellarer. In the early Middle Ages he had been a very important official, whose wide experience often made him an obvious choice for promotion to abbot. By the early fifteenth century he was little more than an administrative 'odd job man'. More and more, economic decisions were taken by the steward, a layman of growing importance in abbey affairs.

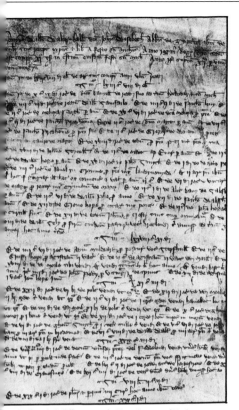

A section from the bailiff's accounts for Tintern's grange of Merthyrgeryn, 1387-88. They record rents, sales, a variety of expenses (e.g. thatching the cow house, 4d; beer given to workers on the new byre, 4d), and provide a vivid impression of the mixed economy here (By kind permission of his grace the Duke of Beaufort; National Library of Wales, Badminton Ms. 1571).

The Black Death, also, often had serious consequences on the number of choir monks. Tintern does not seem to have suffered too severely, and, although there was surely a fall from earlier levels, in 1395 there were fourteen monks plus the abbot.

A new aspect of life at the monastery was the presence of 'corrodians', people who, for one reason or another, spent their old age in the abbey. They included retired abbots, pensioned-off servants, or people who had purchased such a living as security for later life. Tintern was also sent corrodians by a succession of kings from Edward I onwards. They were generally retired royal servants and the obligation was not popular with the abbey for, above all, corrodians would have required accommodation suitable to their former rank.

In 1468, William Herbert became the lord of Chepstow, and a year later was buried at the abbey, following the Battle of Edgecot. In his will he left materials for building work then in progress. A decade later the chronicler and traveller William of Worcester spent several days at Tintern, and made notes on the architecture of the church and other buildings. The appearance of the Wye valley would have been very different from that confronting the first community of the 1130s. Apart from the large monastic complex, a village had emerged beyond the abbey walls. Cottages had been built and even shopkeepers seem to have been present. This was a far cry from the austerity demanded by the early Cistercians.

The Monks at Tintern

Although the initial community of brothers came from the French mother house of L'Aumône, novices were no doubt soon recruited locally. We know the names of some 100 monks over the four centuries, 23 of them rising to be abbots. The most common names were Thomas, William, Walter and Nicholas, as well as the only two Cistercian Edwards known from Wales. Unlike the abbeys in the heart of the Principality, the great majority of Tintern's monks seem to have been of Anglo-Norman or English origin.

Grave slab showing the head of one of Tintern's abbots. This can now be seen in the abbey exhibition. The illustration of about 1820 is by David ap Thomas Powell (By courtesy of Cardiff Central Library).

Dissolution: The End of Monastic Life

In 1521 Richard Wyche was appointed abbot of Tintern, and his was to prove the last abbacy at this noble house. Soon afterwards, monastic life in England and Wales was brought to an abrupt end by the political actions of Henry VIII.

Thomas Cromwell (1485-1540), Henry VIII's Vicar General, responsible for the administration of the Dissolution. A portrait after Hans Holbein (By courtesy of the National Portrait Gallery).

King Henry VIII (1491-1547), from a portrait of about 1536, after Hans Holbein. The Dissolution of the Monasteries was one of the most complicated and drawn out political actions of his reign (By courtesy of the National Portrait Gallery).

king's secretary, Thomas Cromwell, at court. Wyche's reply, begging to be excused for several days in order that he could keep an important feast at the abbey, shows that even then the Cistercian religious life was placed above official business.

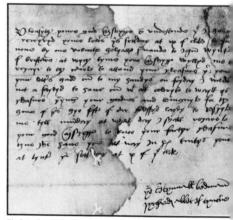

The letter from Richard Wyche, last abbot of Tintern, to Cromwell: 'begging you to respite me till Monday for the honour of this high feast of our Blessed Lady' (Copyright: Public Record Office, SP 1/85/1133).

The Dissolution of the Monasteries was part of the king's policy to establish total control over the Church in his realm. But in addition to severing links with Rome, their suppression was a source of considerable wealth to the crown. Even so, the brutal demise of some 800 religious houses between 1536-40 was a major step, perhaps made easier by a changing tide of opinion against the monasteries and what they stood for. Certainly, by the time of the Tudor dynasty, much of the freshness and vigour of the monastic way of life had been lost.

A precedent had already been set by Cardinal Wolsey, who dissolved almost thirty monasteries in the 1520s, using their income to endow schools and colleges. Rumours were no doubt already circulating when, in September 1534, Richard Wyche received a letter requesting him to visit the

In the following year a survey and valuation of monastic property were made for the king. This *Valor Ecclesiasticus* reveals a net assessed income at Tintern of some £192, though in an Augmentations Survey of 1536 it was valued at £238. Although small by the standards of many English houses, this was sufficient to make the bbey the wealthiest in Wales. Alas, not wealthy nough, for in 1536 an Act was passed dissolving ll religious houses with incomes under £200 per nnum, some two-thirds of the total number. ndeed, the *Valor* figure may have been eliberately falsified to bring Tintern below this hreshold. Even so, the larger houses followed a ew years later.

Tintern Abbey was surrendered to the king's isitors on 3rd September 1536. Apart from Abbot Vyche, there were twelve choir monks and some 5 monastic servants. As they left the abbey walls n that late summer, a way of life which had lasted or 400 years finally came to an end. This time-pan was almost as long as that from the Dissolution itself to our own period.

The abbey silver, plate and ornaments were catalogued, weighed and sent to the king's

treasury. Anything of value was taken away, and in 1537 the site was granted to the earl of Worcester who had succeeded to the lordship of Chepstow through marriage. Generally, the lead was quickly stripped from the roofs and its profits reserved for the king, but at Tintern Henry's plumbers were not melting down the lead until 1541. Eventually, in 1546 part, if not all, of this was bought for £166 by the earl of Worcester, probably for building work at his castles of Chepstow and Raglan.

With the roofs gone, and windows smashed, the shell of the abbey would have fallen into chronic decay. It was more than two centuries before the glories of Tintern were once again appreciated, and we shall pick up this story following our examination of the medieval buildings.

Following the Dissolution Tintern, like most other monasteries, gradually fell into a state of chronic decay. This lithograph, of about 1850, shows the east nd of the abbey church (By courtesy of the National Library of Wales).

II Masons at Work:
The Development of the Buildings

Almost every large monastic house had a long and complex building history, often spread over the entire Middle Ages. At Tintern building campaigns were to span the four centuries from foundation to dissolution. Few monks can have succeeded in spending their monastic life free from the necessity of avoiding masons' scaffolding in one or other part of the monastery.

During the early Middle Ages, part of the building work at Cistercian abbeys may have been undertaken by the lay brothers. This is a rather more spiritual impression of monks building with angelic help, from a manuscript produced at Benedictine Durham about 1190-1200 (Copyright: The British Library, Additional Ms. 39943, f. 39).

The Cistercian Plan

All Cistercian monasteries were laid out according to a distinct plan (see coloured plan at the back of this guide), reflecting the centralized organization of the order itself. In general they followed the customary medieval monastic outline, which was practical and made the best possible use of natural light. This plan was composed of three main elements. The most important of these was the *church*, the focus of the spiritual and physical life of the monastery. This was generally orientated east — west, and at Tintern lay at the southern end of the complex. The second element comprised the conventual

buildings in which the community lived, ate, conducted administration, cared for their sick and old, and provided hospitality for guests. These were laid out around an open square or *cloister*, which at Tintern lay to the north of the church, with a secondary block arranged around a lesser cloister to the north-east. The third and final element was made up of those structures serving the daily needs of the monastery at large, and also providing facilities for the exploitation of outlying estates. These would have included barns, stables, a brewhouse, bakehouse, mill, dairy and so on, and were normally located in an area adjacent to the church and cloister known as the *outer court*. At Tintern this was west of the abbey, next to the modern car park, and has been the subject of recent archaeological investigation.

The major distinctions between the Cistercian plan and that of the earlier Benedictine monks, stemmed from the need to accommodate large numbers of lay brethren. A distinct place was reserved for their exclusive use in the monastic church, and the western range of the cloister was usually given over to their domestic use, as at Tintern.

The Twelfth-Century Abbey

The Cistercian constitution required the founder of a new monastery to provide some form of buildings before the arrival of the monks. These may have been temporary, but were to include at least a church, a dining hall, a dormitory, a guest-house and a porter's lodge. Excavations have shown that these early buildings were often of wood. Moreover, on many sites, even when stone construction began in earnest, many buildings remained of wood for several centuries.

Lay Brothers'
(West) Range

**An Impression of Tintern Abbey as it m[...]
have Appeared in the Late Twelfth Cen[...]**

Sketch Plan of the Abbey in the Twelfth Century

Initial buildings
Late twelfth-century additions

Latrine

Lay Brothers' Range

Kitchen

Dining Hall

Dormitory (above)

Chapter House

Cloister

N

Nave

Presbytery

CHURCH

Feet 0   20   40   60   80   100

We cannot be sure if the earliest structures provided by Walter fitz Richard at Tintern were of wood, but work in stone progressed quickly after the foundation, and a church and several domestic ranges were completed probably before 1160. Very little of these survives above ground, and the plan of the church has only been recovered through excavation. In this period, and throughout Tintern's history, the cloister was positioned north of the church, and this in itself was something of an anomaly. Cloisters were usually placed to the south, thereby making good use of natural light. At Tintern, however, the provision of an adequate water supply and drainage seems to have dictated otherwise (pp.38-9).

The twelfth-century abbey was laid out on modest scale. The church was cruciform (cross-shaped), with a small presbytery (east end); transepts to the north and south, with two chapels to the east of each; and a narrow aisleless nave. It was just 165 feet (50m) in length. A domestic range, with a chapter house where the monks met for daily administrative business (pp.40-1), and a first-floor dormitory, adjoined the north transept. The dining hall probably ran east – west, parallel with the church, and with a kitchen at its western end. The plan of the lay brothers' range at this stage has not been recovered, but it may well have been completed in stone during the twelfth century, and possibly projected north of the cloister.

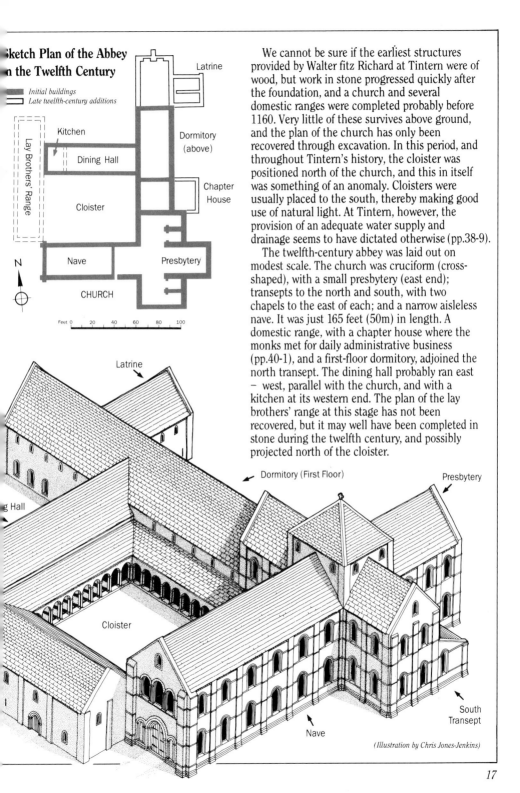

Latrine

g Hall

Dormitory (First Floor)

Presbytery

Cloister

Nave

South Transept

(Illustration by Chris Jones-Jenkins)

17

We should not be misled by the small scale of these early buildings, since they would have been comfortable and adequate for the fledgling community. The church compared well with the sister house at Waverley, with its total length of 180 feet (55m), and with the earliest church recently excavated at Fountains, Yorkshire, measuring just 135 feet (41m). All three were built before the influence of centralized Cistercian planning (especially the *Bernardine* church plan) arrived in this country. They represent the features required in any small monastic church of the period, and parallels can even be found outside the order.

In all, we can get some impression of twelfth-century Tintern by looking at French Cistercian monasteries such as Bernay and Fontenay in Burgundy, or Senanque in Provence. The modest romanesque church would have had small round-headed windows and perhaps, before the end of the century, a low tower may have been added over the central crossing. The interior would have echoed the austerity of the early Cistercians, with plain walls and perhaps a wooden or simple barrel-shaped roof or vault.

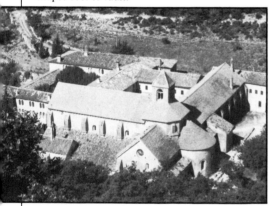

Sénanque Abbey, Provence, southern France. Founded in 1148, its surviving twelfth-century church and claustral buildings provide a reasonable impression of the nature of Tintern in this period (By courtesy of the French Government Tourist Office).

Tintern drew sufficient recruits in the twelfth century to allow the colonization of two daughter houses. The growing number of monks was also reflected in further building before 1200. The dormitory was extended northwards, and a spacious latrine block added. The chapter house was also extended beyond the width of the range, again reflecting the need to accommodate a larger body of monks.

Rebuilding the Cloister Ranges (*c.*1220-60)

With these increasing numbers, want of space would have demanded enlargement of the twelfth-century domestic buildings. By 1220 the abbey was ready to go ahead, and a major programme of work was begun on all three domestic ranges around the cloister.

From about 1150, it had become Cistercian practice to build their dining halls at right angles to the cloister, thereby providing space for other rooms to the east and west. The new work at Tintern began with a larger dining hall, extending

ell north of the original range (pp.45-6). In the space created to the east, a warming house was inserted; one of the few places in the abbey where a fire was kept burning in the winter months. To the west, a kitchen was built where it could serve the monks in the new dining hall, as well as the lay brothers' range to its opposite side.

This kitchen also opened into a completely rebuilt west range intended for the lay brothers, with dining accommodation below and a dormitory above. Cellarage or storage space was provided at the southern end, and there was probably an apartment for the cellarer himself, whose duty it was to oversee the lay brothers.

The north range of the cloister at Tintern, showing the entrance to the dining hall as it appears today.

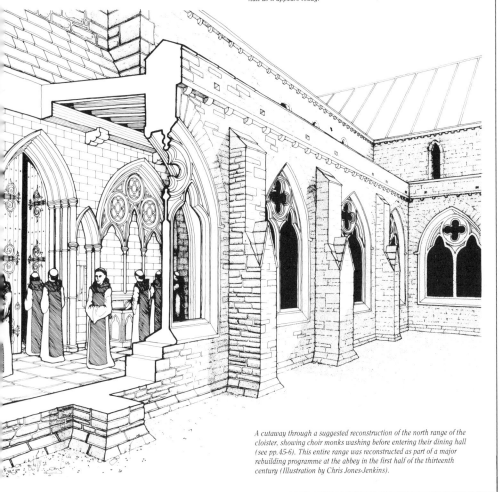

A cutaway through a suggested reconstruction of the north range of the cloister, showing choir monks washing before entering their dining hall (see pp.45-6). This entire range was reconstructed as part of a major rebuilding programme at the abbey in the first half of the thirteenth century (Illustration by Chris Jones-Jenkins).

As this work was progressing, so too was a complete refurbishment of the east range. The chapter house, extended in the late twelfth century, was now refashioned in the style of the period. The doorway from the cloister was given three openings with richly clustered pillars, and a new vaulted roof was inserted. The northern end of the range was much modified. The ground floor here had been given over to the novice monks, and their large hall was now given up-to-date windows and a fine stone vault supported on central pillars. This work, and that in the chapter house, must have caused a good deal of disturbance in the monks' dormitory above.

At least two other buildings were constructed at Tintern during the earlier thirteenth century, outside the cloister area, slightly to the north-east. The building nearest the cloister lay east of the monks' latrine, and was probably attached to it at first floor level. It seems likely that this was intended as the abbot's apartment. Although Cistercian custom required the abbot to sleep in the common dormitory, by this time, in many monasteries, they were acquiring separate lodgings. The attachment to the dormitory, via the latrine, meant that technically, at least, he was under the same roof.

The second building, also of two storeys, lay detached from the remainder of the abbey. Similar free-standing blocks have sometimes been interpreted as accommodation for the abbot of the mother house on his regular visits to the daughter colony. This was perhaps the case here, and the abbot of L'Aumône may have used this building on occasions. Gradually, however, it seems to have provided additional rooms for the abbot of Tintern himself (p.50).

The footings of the once free-standing block to the north-east of the abbey complex. Built in the early thirteenth century, it may have been intended as a visiting abbot's house. Later the abbot of Tintern occupied this himself, with his chapel situated on the first floor of the now taller fourteenth-century addition to the left (see pp.50-1).

Sketch Plan of the Abbey in the Early Thirteenth Century

Below: Remains of one of the pillars inserted to support a new stone vault in the novices' lodging (east range) during the earlier thirteenth century (Illustration by Delyth Lloyd).

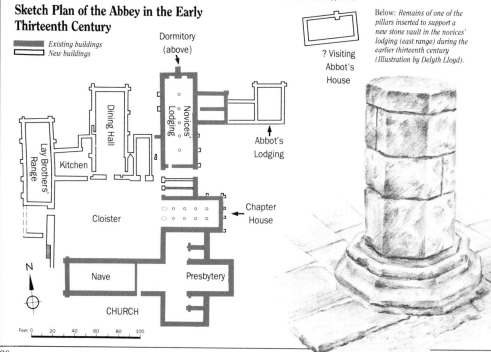

Domestic Building in the Later Thirteenth Century

The rebuilding work, begun about 1220, must have continued almost without pause throughout the earlier thirteenth century, and the abbey masons were kept busy with further additions to the domestic structures before 1300.

Tintern seems to have continued to attract growing numbers of lay brethren. As a result, before the close of the century, it was necessary to

The most significant new domestic building at this time was the infirmary, the place in the monastery for sick and aged monks. It seems probable that the new infirmary replaced an

Seal of the abbot of Tintern, dating to 1256, at which time much reconstruction work was still in progress. An abbot in a chasuble, holds a pastoral staff in his right hand, and a book in his left. The legend reads: +SIG[ ]BATIS . DE. TIN[ ] (By permission of the National Museum of Wales).

Sketch Plan of the Abbey in the Later Thirteenth Century

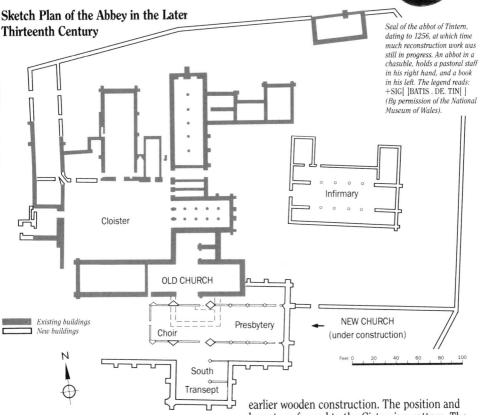

Infirmary

Cloister

OLD CHURCH

Existing buildings
New buildings

Presbytery
Choir

NEW CHURCH
(under construction)

Feet 0   20   40   60   80   100

N

South
Transept

extend their building northwards. This extension was at least a third of the size of the original range, and can be identified from a distinct change in the character of the external masonry. An addition was also made to the southern end of the west range at this time. A porch was constructed around the small gateway where visitors from outside would have approached the cloister.

earlier wooden construction. The position and layout conformed to the Cistercian pattern. The completion of the building resulted in a second cloister enclosure, outside the other main domestic ranges.

The interior of the infirmary was similar to a modern hospital ward, with a large hall, divided into a nave and aisles by two rows of columns. The beds would have been between the columns in each aisle. This arrangement was considerably modified in the later Middle Ages.

A New Church (*c.*1269-1301)

The most prominent work of the later thirteenth century was the raising of a magnificent new church. In scale, grandeur and lavishness, it dwarfed the first simple romanesque church, and went well beyond the austerity of the early Cistercians.

A now lost chronicle records that in 1301, *'the new church of Tintern Abbey, thirty-two years in building, was finished by Roger Bigod'*. If this is accurate, the decision to rebuild was taken in 1269. The completion of the new church on such a scale, and in a comparatively short time-span, was due to the patronage of Earl Roger Bigod. His arms were eventually emblazoned in the large window above the high altar, and in the fifteenth century William of Worcester named him as builder of the church of Tintern.

The new church is likely to have been planned as a whole, and was laid out slightly south of the existing edifice. Building advanced in such a way that the monks could continue to use their first church until the eastern part of the new building was sufficiently complete to allow the transfer of the main high altar services. Thus, the thirteenth-century church grew as a shell, eventually encasing its much smaller predecessor. Enough progress had been made by 1282 to permit the celebration of mass at the high altar, and by 1288 the choir monks were able to take possession of their part of the new building. At this stage, if not before, this would have meant the dismantling of the old south transept, in order that the monks could gain access from their dormitory to the north. During the work we must imagine a busy scene with scaffolding, temporary wooden screens, barrow runs (p.36), stone dust, semi-glazed windows and half completed vaults. In the midst of it all the monks must have found it difficult to retain the tranquillity of their religious life.

As work progressed to the west, towards the lay brothers' section of the church, there seems to have been a break at some point in the construction. The key to this is in the detail around certain of the southern windows. In particular, the interested visitor will notice that, in the earlier stages of the work, detached shafts were placed in the jambs or slight recesses at either side of the inner window edge, and these have now all disappeared. Later stages of work are

Clerestory windows on the south side of the nave. Notice the absence of the once detached shafts in the jambs of the window to the east (A). Those to the west (B) have attached shafts, marking the beginning of the second building period on the new church.

marked by attached shafts which can still be seen today. In addition, a further indication is given by the two windows in the extreme south-west of the church, both of which are smaller than the earlier examples to the east. The exact position of the

Roger Bigod's great church grew as a shell around the twelfth-century building. This imaginative scene conveys how difficult it must have been to retain the tranquility of monastic life at Tintern during this time. Construction began about 1269, and by 1288 the work was sufficiently advanced for the choir monks to take possession of the eastern end. The old church had to be pulled down before the west end could be finally completed.

break in construction can be traced on the coloured plan at the back of this guide.

Before the final stages of work could be completed the nave of the twelfth-century church would have had to be pulled down. This done, the cloister area would have been considerably extended. Despite the evidence of the lost chronicle, work probably extended well into the fourteenth century. As late as 1340 there is mention in documents of 'the Keeper of the Work of the church of Tintern'. One of the last parts to see completion was the north transept, where a section of walling from the first church was also retained. Just west of this transept, the elaborate processional doorway into the church also belongs to these final stages.

The completed church measured some 236 feet (72m) in total length. This was virtually identical in scale with the rebuilt church at Neath Abbey, constructed in much the same period. Both reflect fashions preferred in Cistercian houses during the mid to late thirteenth century, especially in the extended eastern end and in the emphasis upon a large east window.

The Later Middle Ages

Although most major building campaigns at Tintern ended with the completion of the church, other structures were added and modified throughout the later Middle Ages.

During the fourteenth century a small courtyard was built at the southern end of the west range. This may have served as a cloister for the lay brothers. To the east of the site, a covered passage was inserted to connect the new church with the infirmary. The greatest undertaking in this century, however, was concerned with extensions and improvements to the abbot's lodging (pp.50-1). An imposing new hall was built above a cellared undercroft. Cistercian abbots everywhere had become magnates of considerable local consequence, but the grand scale of this hall at Tintern was quite exceptional. Additions were also made to the older thirteenth-century block in this area. A private chapel was built in a two-storey extension to the south, with access at first floor level, and a latrine and even a dovecot were added to the east. At least two other chambers were erected to the south of the abbot's complex during the fourteenth century.

The following century was to witness many minor alterations to existing abbey buildings. Although it is difficult to identify them precisely, we can be sure that a number of private rooms were created for senior monks, and apartments are

Sketch Plan of the Abbey in the Later Middle Ages

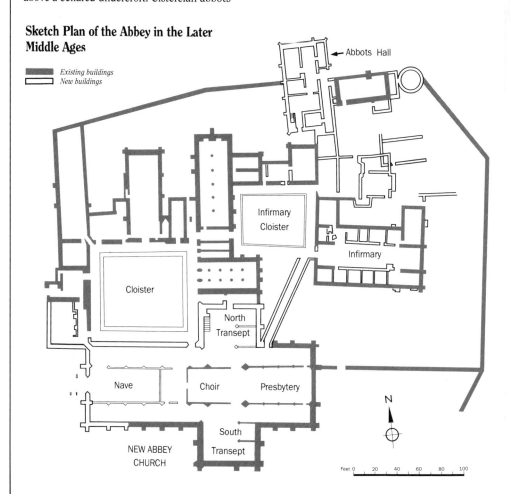

Existing buildings
New buildings

Abbots Hall

Infirmary Cloister

Infirmary

Cloister

North Transept

Nave   Choir   Presbytery

N

South Transept

NEW ABBEY CHURCH

Feet 0   20   40   60   80   100

likely to have been provided for several of the corrodians which the house found it necessary to support in the later Middle Ages. The earlier abbot's house, adjacent to the monks' latrine block, for example, is one building which was perhaps utilized in this way.

Somewhat easier to pin-point are the changes which took place in the infirmary (pp.48-9). The aisles within the main hall were possibly partitioned off with wooden screens at an early date, but they were now separated from the

Indications of progress with the late fifteenth-century rebuilding in the cloister alleys can be seen, around the earlier processional doorway, in the south-east corner.

The south alley of the late fourteenth-century cloisters at the Benedictine abbey of Gloucester, now the cathedral. Tintern is unlikely to have had the resources for quite such a construction, but may have been aspiring to similar levels of comfort (Illustration by Delyth Lloyd).

central nave of the building by solid stone walls. Each aisle was then divided into individual rooms, each with its own fireplace. The infirmary kitchen was also rebuilt and extended during the fifteenth century, and this suggests improvements to the diet of the sick and elderly brothers.

Altogether, these works reflect an updating of conditions within existing abbey buildings; they show a trend towards a demand for better and more modern standards of living. In turn, this demonstrates something of the significant changes which had taken place within the Cistercian life. The lay brothers had ceased to be a major force; much of the early austerity had gone, and even a meat diet had been sanctioned for all monks.

Such improvements to abbey comforts were not, however, the only building programmes undertaken in later centuries. In particular, by the early fifteenth century, Tintern had become something of a pilgrimage centre, with a venerated statue of the Virgin Mary. The statue (which may be that now preserved in the exhibition hall) was located in a chapel outside the west door of the abbey church, but all traces of this have now disappeared. Nevertheless, although only a few column bases remain as evidence, we know of an elaborate fifteenth-century porch added to the west front. The chapel could well have been constructed in the same period, and located as an upper floor above the porch.

The fifteenth century saw various attempts to improve the covered walks around the main cloister. To begin with, in 1411-12 the monks tried to repair the existing roof, but later in the century an ambitious complete rebuilding was contemplated. Indeed, in 1469 William Herbert bequeathed 100 tons of stone to the monastery for restoration of its cloister. A certain amount of progress was certainly made, and there are indications as to its appearance in the south-east corner. It could well have been planned after the same fashion as the superb cloisters executed somewhat earlier at Gloucester Abbey (now the cathedral), but those at Tintern were probably never completed (p.38-9).

Taken as a whole, we should now appreciate just how extensive the building work at a medieval monastery could be. To many of the monks who spent their lives at Tintern, the sound of the mason's hammer must have been almost as familiar as their own singing in the choir.

III The Abbey at Work:
A Tour of the Buildings

Ideally, in order fully to appreciate the abbey at work, we should follow the path of a Cistercian monk through a 'typical' monastic day, but this would be difficult and time-consuming. Instead, one guided route is offered the visitor in the following pages.

The suggested tour begins with the major survival: the monastic church of Tintern. From there, we progress to the three main domestic ranges of buildings around the cloister, and finally to those structures north and east of the smaller infirmary cloister.

Originally, entrance to the buildings would have been through the thirteenth-century porch and the outer parlour at the southern end of the lay brothers' range. Today, visitors arrive through the modern ticket office and exhibition complex to the north of the site. They enter the abbey buildings along the northern range of the cloister, and from there may proceed to the church.

The Church

We may begin our tour outside the main west door into the abbey church. The decorated stonework in the wall panels, together with that which survives in the great seven-light window, makes a beautiful composition and is fairly typical of the later thirteenth to early fourteenth centuries. The almond-shaped niche above the mullion of the central doorway is likely to have housed a carved figure of St Mary. To the front of this west door, the column bases are the only survivals of the porch added here in the fifteenth century. This arcaded construction possibly supported the chapel containing the revered statue of Our Lady (p.25). The elevated position of such a pilgrimage chapel would partially have blocked the lower sections of the west window.

The composition of this west front presented a fitting image for the monks as they approached on their regular Sunday processions through the abbey. Following the monks, we now enter the church via the west door.

One is now inside Tintern's magnificent second church, built slightly to the south of the earlier

edifice. The difference in scale and position between the two is best appreciated by observing and pacing out the foundations of the first church, which are clearly marked out on the ground.

Rising around these slight traces, Roger Bigod's church remains remarkably complete. Apart from the roof, and the stone tracery and glass from the windows, the most obvious things missing are the pillars of the arcade on the north side of the nave. Nevertheless, we should be aware that its detailed appearance is very different from that which would have been encountered during the Middle Ages.

Left: *The west front of the abbey church, completed in the early fourteenth century.*

Below: *The interior of the abbey church, looking south-east along the full length of the nave towards the choir and presbytery.*

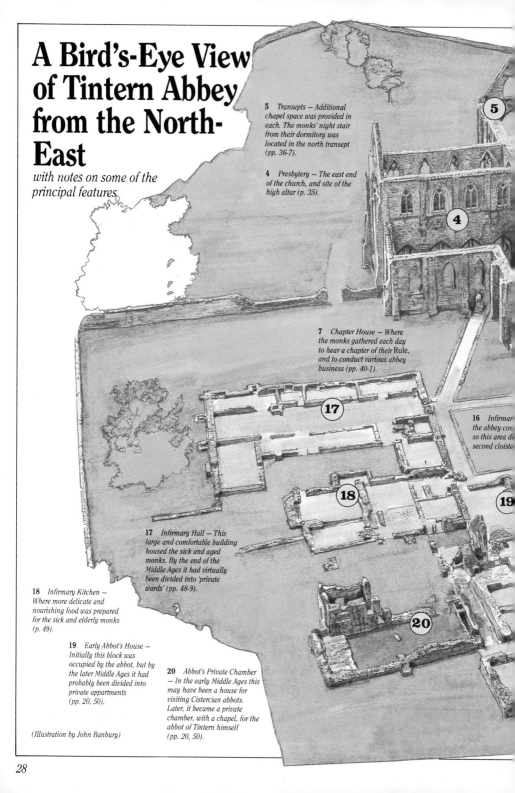

A Bird's-Eye View of Tintern Abbey from the North-East

with notes on some of the principal features

5 Transepts – Additional chapel space was provided in each. The monks' night stair from their dormitory was located in the north transept (pp. 36-7).

4 Presbytery – The east end of the church, and site of the high altar (p. 35).

5

4

7 Chapter House – Where the monks gathered each day to hear a chapter of their Rule, and to conduct various abbey business (pp. 40-1).

17

16 Infirmar the abbey co. so this area d second cloiste

18

19

17 Infirmary Hall – This large and comfortable building housed the sick and aged monks. By the end of the Middle Ages it had virtually been divided into 'private wards' (pp. 48-9).

18 Infirmary Kitchen – Where more delicate and nourishing food was prepared for the sick and elderly monks (p. 49).

19 Early Abbot's House – Initially this block was occupied by the abbot, but by the later Middle Ages it had probably been divided into private appartments (pp. 20, 50).

20 Abbot's Private Chamber – In the early Middle Ages this may have been a house for visiting Cistercian abbots. Later, it became a private chamber, with a chapel, for the abbot of Tintern himself (pp. 20, 50).

20

(Illustration by John Banbury)

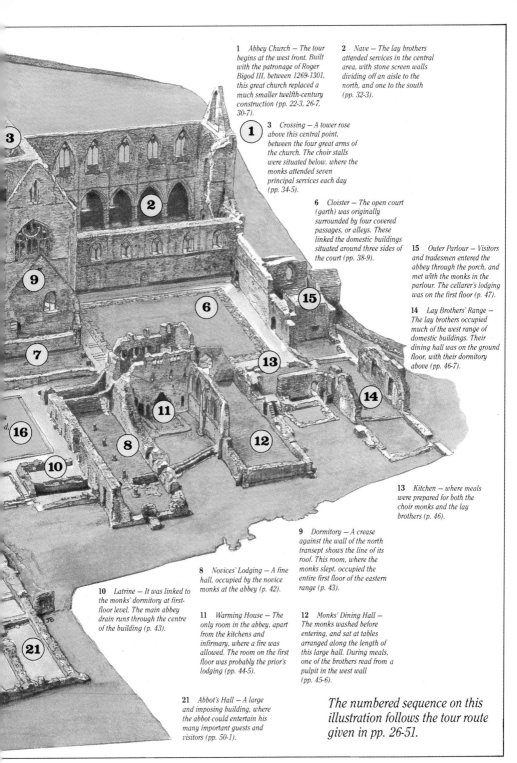

1 Abbey Church – The tour begins at the west front. Built with the patronage of Roger Bigod III, between 1269-1301, this great church replaced a much smaller twelfth-century construction (pp. 22-3, 26-7, 30-7).

2 Nave – The lay brothers attended services in the central area, with stone screen walls dividing off an aisle to the north, and one to the south (pp. 32-3).

3 Crossing – A tower rose above this central point, between the four great arms of the church. The choir stalls were situated below, where the monks attended seven principal services each day (pp. 34-5).

6 Cloister – The open court (garth) was originally surrounded by four covered passages, or alleys. These linked the domestic buildings situated around three sides of the court (pp. 38-9).

15 Outer Parlour – Visitors and tradesmen entered the abbey through the porch, and met with the monks in the parlour. The cellarer's lodging was on the first floor (p. 47).

14 Lay Brothers' Range – The lay brothers occupied much of the west range of domestic buildings. Their dining hall was on the ground floor, with their dormitory above (pp. 46-7).

13 Kitchen – where meals were prepared for both the choir monks and the lay brothers (p. 46).

9 Dormitory – A crease against the wall of the north transept shows the line of its roof. This room, where the monks slept, occupied the entire first floor of the eastern range (p. 43).

8 Novices' Lodging – A fine hall, occupied by the novice monks at the abbey (p. 42).

10 Latrine – It was linked to the monks' dormitory at first-floor level. The main abbey drain runs through the centre of the building (p. 43).

11 Warming House – The only room in the abbey, apart from the kitchens and infirmary, where a fire was allowed. The room on the first floor was probably the prior's lodging (pp. 44-5).

12 Monks' Dining Hall – The monks washed before entering, and sat at tables arranged along the length of this large hall. During meals, one of the brothers read from a pulpit in the west wall (pp. 45-6).

21 Abbot's Hall – A large and imposing building, where the abbot could entertain his many important guests and visitors (pp. 50-1).

The numbered sequence on this illustration follows the tour route given in pp. 26-51.

Decoration: Rethinking the Internal Appearance

It is important to understand that the interior of the church was never meant to be seen or used as a whole. It was, from the first, divided up to suit the ritual arrangement of the Cistercian order. Stone screen walls, some nine feet (2.7m) high, ran between the two rows of arcade pillars along the entire length of the church, thereby dividing the central portion from an aisle at either side. In turn, this centrally screened section was divided across its width by further stone partition walls. In this way several distinct areas were created for specific allocation and functions.

Turning to the walls themselves, there would in medieval times have been a fair degree of decoration and an altogether brighter appearance. Very little of the red sandstone now exposed was originally left bare. Surviving fragments tell us that the walls were covered in plaster, which was probably coloured, and had imitation joints depicted by red lines. By the later Middle Ages there were perhaps scenes of greater elaboration painted at prominent positions. Such decoration complemented the sheen from the church floor, large areas of which were paved in richly decorated tiles. These primarily red glazed pavements carried a selection of heraldic and symmetrical designs picked out by white clay. It is difficult to appreciate the overall effect they created, but a general impression of the appearance will be gained by studying examples of individual tiles in the abbey exhibition.

The roof requires more imagination to visualize. Standing at the centre, one may notice at a level just above the arches of the aisle arcades, a series of delicate vertical triple shafts carried on corbels and extending along the full length of the church. These support the splayed 'springers', which took the weight of the vaults. The church had stone vaulted ceilings throughout with simple diagonal and transverse ribs. There were large bosses at the intersections of the diagonal ribs, examples of which have been laid out in the south aisle. The whole was almost certainly painted, particularly the leaflike designs of the bosses, but the entire vault was probably later in date than the main walls. When the vaults were in position there would have been a large amount of space between the tops of the vaults and the external roofs. These 'attic' areas were lit by the great windows

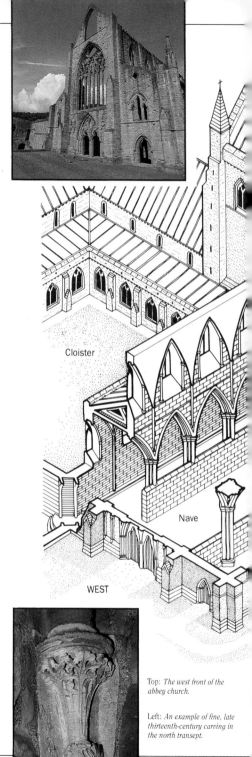

Top: *The west front of the abbey church.*

Left: *An example of fine, late thirteenth-century carving in the north transept.*

NORTH

EAST

Presbytery

Choir

South
Transept

SOUTH

Aisle

South

**Cutaway Reconstruction
of the Abbey Church
from the South-West**

*This suggested reconstruction shows how the interior of the building was
originally divided up by solid screen walls, to suit the ritual arrangements of
the Cistercians (Illustration by Chris Jones-Jenkins).*

that survive in all four gables of the church.
Stairways at several points gave access to these
spaces.

Finally, before leaving considerations of internal
decoration and appearance, we should not
overlook the numerous tombs situated in many
parts of the church by the time of the Dissolution.
There are tantalizing hints, such as the effigy of a

knight in chain armour dating to about 1240-50
(see illustration p.11), that benefactors often
required elaborate burial rites within the abbey.
Unfortunately, most traces are now gone, and we
cannot be sure if the few tombstones which
survive today are in their original positions. One
possible candidate is that under the north arch of
the crossing to a Nicholas of Llandaff, possibly the
treasurer of the cathedral there from 1196-1218. It
lay in the south transept of the first church, but
was buried underneath the floor of Roger Bigod's
new building. Other tombstones can be seen in
the south aisle and south transept.

The Nave: the Lay Brothers' Church

The aisled nave consists of six bays (a bay being the space between each pair of pillars) and most of it survives, apart from the north arcade. This had collapsed well before the turn of the nineteenth century, and the south arcade was just saved from a similar fate by a system of steel reinforcing. This work was done in the early part of the present century, at which time a new roof was placed over the south aisle. The majority of the nave was initially devoted to the lay brethren.

The central part of the four westernmost bays was screened off from the remainder, and it was here that the lay brothers attended services. They entered the church, from their quarters in the western range, through a doorway set diagonally in the far north-west corner. From here, a gap left in the first bay of the northern screen wall allowed access to their central choir. Within this choir the lay brothers occupied stalls, or seats, which backed against the partition walls at either side of the second and third bays. Their high altar was centrally situated in front of a further screen crossing the church between the fourth pair of pillars. This particular screen is likely to have supported the carved figures of the rood or crucifixion.

Behind this, the fifth bay, with openings in the partition walls to both the north and south aisles, served as the retro-choir. This was the place in the church where aged and infirm monks were allowed to sit during the offices. The retro-choir was enclosed by yet another screen probably linking the next pair of pillars. This was known as the *pulpitum*, and was the major divide between the nave and the eastern end of the church. It was richly decorated with stone panelling and survived, in part, until the mid nineteenth century

The nave, or lay brothers' section of the abbey church, seen through the west doorway into the south aisle. Notice the stubs of the screen walls, originally linking the arcade pillars, and dividing up the interior.

The remains of the pulpitum can be seen running across the width of the nave in this late nineteenth-century photograph. Various dressed fragments have been heaped against it, but the base of the central doorway is clear.

varying design, located in each bay. On the southern side, these were all of two lights, but the two at the far west were smaller than the others in this aisle. This probably reflects stylistic changes in the second phase of building the church during the later thirteenth century, but may also indicate a temporary shortage of funds. The north aisle windows also belong to the second phase of construction, and these too, are shorter and also of two lights. In this case the high sills would have been necessary to clear the roof of the covered cloister walk outside (p.38-9).

The last bay in this northern aisle is even later in date, and it contains the east processional doorway through which the choir monks entered the church from the cloister. This is best appreciated by stepping outside briefly to examine the sumptuous fourteenth century carving around its frame, and the large trefoil above.

The early fourteenth-century processional doorway from the cloister into the nave of the abbey church (Illustration by Delyth Lloyd).

when it was removed to provide a full vista along the ruins. The *pulpitum* probably stood to at least ten feet (3m) and had a doorway at the centre, with a stairway to a loft above. Sometimes organs were placed on such lofts in monastic churches.

Retracing our steps a little, we must bear in mind that the nave aisles at this time served only as passages linking the eastern and western ends of the church. Cut off as they were from the central nave, the aisles were lit by windows, of

The south aisle of the nave, showing the smaller windows in the two later westernmost bays (see also p.23).

Before leaving the nave, it is ironic to think that soon after its construction the lay brothers ceased to be a significant force at Tintern. Thus, their special allocation within the church was no longer required. We can only really guess at the subsequent use of the nave. Even so, the rood screen was probably retained, and it seems likely that the western bays were only used regularly for processions. As at other Cistercian houses, some of the bays in the north and south aisles may have been converted to chapels. This would have facilitated the increasingly usual practice in the later Middle Ages of each choir monk offering a daily mass. In addition, such chapels could be used for the remembrance of benefactors.

The Monks' Choir and Presbytery

From immediately east of the *pulpitum*, almost to the far eastern end of the church, the centrally screened off area was occupied by the monks' choir and presbytery. By virtue of the screen walls, it may be thought of as a church set within the abbey church, and it was the focus of all the principal services of the monks. At the west end were the stalls of the choir monks, while at the east, just in front of the last pair of pillars in the presbytery, stood the high altar. Access was gained either through the door in the *pulpitum* from the west, or through a break in the screen wall facing the north transept.

The choir extended from the last bay of the nave, into the crossing. The latter was the central area between the four arms of the church. Here, the massive multi-clustered pillars rise to support four great arches, above which presumably rose a

Right: *The two massive southern pillars of the crossing, looking eastwards from the nave. The clustered shafts on the nearer (west) pillar are not carried to the ground, thereby allowing room for the back of the monks' choir stalls.*

Below: *The crossing, looking west, from the position of the high altar. This was the central area, situated between the four great arms of the church. The arches rose to support a central tower, and situated below were the monks' choir stalls.*

carried down to the ground, therby allowing room for the choir stalls at this point.

The presbytery occupied the three bays from the crossing towards the east of the church, and was approached via at least one step up from the choir. In the north and south arcades of each bay, the clustered pillars rise to arches, above which a blank level is divided by two string-courses. The whole is surmounted by clerestory windows above the level of the aisle roofs. The high altar was in the last bay in front of another solid stone wall across the church. Towering above, separated by a single bay, was the great east window. Originally of eight lights, this has lost most of its stone tracery, but is known to have been filled with painted glass, some bearing the arms of the 'second founder', Roger Bigod. With the sun streaming in from the east, this must have been a glorious sight.

A reconstruction of the tracery in the great east window. A detail taken from Edmund Sharpe's, Architectural Parallels (London 1848).

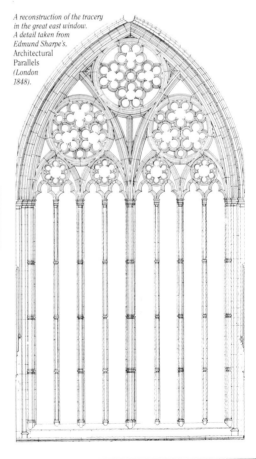

Cistercian monks sat in their choir stalls, with one of their brethren kneeling at the high altar. Taken from a psalter of about 1430 (Copyright: The British Library, Cotton Domitian Ms. A XVII, f. 150v).

squat central tower, typical of Cistercian churches, and containing several bells.

During the seven major services of the day, the monks would have sat in their choir stalls. These were probably arranged in two or three tiers and made of richly carved oak. They are likely to have backed along the *pulpitum* and, as in the lay brothers' church, also faced inwards backing against the side screen walls. The clustered shafts on the two western pillars of the crossing are not

The Eastern Aisles or Processional Walk

The north, south and eastern aisles in this part of the church were cut off from the presbytery by the screen walls. They served as a processional walk, part of the route between the north and south transepts. Against the eastern wall stood four lesser altars, two behind the high altar on a raised platform which is still in position, and one in each aisle. There were breaks in the north and south screens of the last bay to allow the passage of processions. There was a three-light window in the east wall of the aisles, and a two-light window in each bay.

In the last bay of the south aisle the recess in the outer wall may have contained a piscina, or small basin used to cleanse the sacramental vessels. In the middle of the east wall, below the great window, is a low blocked arch indicating a barrow way used by the builders during the construction of the church. Finally, at the western

Blocked arch below the great east window, indicating a barrow way probably used by the builders during the construction of the church. The plinth in the foreground supported two altars situated in chapels against this wall (Illustration by John Banbury).

end of the north aisle is a doorway which gave access to the passage leading to the infirmary. This was one of the last parts to be built since it lay within the east end of the first church. A break in the masonry can be identified east of this doorway.

The South and North Transepts

The south and north transepts formed the two cross arms of the abbey church. They are of similar design, with a broad western part rising to the full height of the church, and a lower eastern aisle divided into chapels.

The visitor may wish to turn to the south transept first. The end wall is pierced by a very tall window, originally of six lights, which has lost all of its tracery. Beneath is a doorway, with a gable extending into the lower part of the window. This doorway was used for processional purposes, and probably gave access to the monks' cemetery. In the south-east angle a circular stairway led to a gallery in the west wall, as well as to the roofs.

The south transept, looking towards its large end window, which was originally of six lights. Through the arcade to the left (east) lay the two transept chapels.

The east wall is of precisely similar design to the arcade of the presbytery. Through this, the two eastern chapels were separated from each other, and from the presbytery aisle, by screen walls. The base of an altar survives in the northern chapel.

The northern chapel in the south transept, with the remains of its altar surviving below the window (Illustration by Delyth Lloyd).

In the north transept is a similar arrangement, but because the first church occupied its site, it is of various dates. The end wall is again pierced by a large six-light window, retaining much of its stone tracery. Interestingly, the glass was never carried all the way down, as the roof of the monks' dormitory abutted against the exterior wall of the transept. As a result, the lower parts of the window were simply treated as wall panelling.

The north transept, with the monks' night stairs down from their dormitory in the left-hand corner (By courtesy of the Royal Commission on Ancient and Historical Monuments, Wales).

In the north-west corner was the night stair. The existing steps are modern, but they are built on the line of the original ones and lead to a doorway through which the monks entered the church from their dormitory for services at night. Also in this corner, as in the south transept, is a circular stair leading this time from dormitory level to a wall gallery and the roof spaces.

Reconstruction of the night stairs in the north transept, with the monks descending to attend a service in their choir (Illustration by Chris Jones-Jenkins).

To the east of the night stairs, the doorway at ground level led to the sacristy or vestry, the room for keeping the sacred vessels and vestments used in services (p.40). The eastern chapels were again divided from each other by screen walls, with the base of an altar surviving in the northern one of the two. Some of the original wall plaster can be seen surviving in this area. From this point, looking high up at the east wall of the transept, we can observe the abutments for two flying buttresses, a feature that does not occur elsewhere at Tintern.

From the north transept, we may now progress from the church, through the processional doorway in the north aisle of the nave, out into the monastic cloister.

The Cloister

If the church was the spiritual focus of the abbey, the cloister was the centre of domestic life. There was much toing and froing in this area throughout the monastic day.

For reasons already outlined, the cloister at Tintern lay to the north, otherwise the buildings around the square conform closely to the normal Cistercian plan. The cloister was originally built to accompany the first church; it was enlarged in the thirteenth century, and in the late fifteenth century a further rebuilding was begun.

A view across the cloister from the north. The now open square was originally surrounded by a covered passage, or alley, on each side.

As completed, the square measured some 100 by 110 feet (30 x 33m). The central open court, or garth, was surrounded by four covered passages known as alleys. During the early Middle Ages, the sides facing the garth probably had open arcades, leaving the alleys cold and cheerless in Winter, but windows may have been added in later centuries. A large number of the corbels which carried the lean-to roofs can be seen in the surrounding walls. On the south and west sides, these can clearly be identified on two levels, and

The line of the lean-to roofs in the south-west corner of the cloister garth, with supporting stone corbels at two levels (Illustration by John Banbury).

probably indicate changes, or at least planned changes, in the roofs. Also on these two sides there are clear indications of a thickening in the outer walls of the cloister walk. The wider

Indications of a thickening in the outer wall of the west cloister walk, possibly intended to support a more elaborate fifteenth-century alley.

foundations may have been intended for the newly planned alleys of the fifteenth century. Indeed, those to the south could well have been intended to accommodate carrells, or individual cubicles where the monks could undertake private study.

The cloister not only provided covered access between the various parts of the abbey, but was also used by the monks for study, particularly the alley next to the church. Indeed, Tintern possesses a rare Cistercian feature associated with these periods of study, and especially with that known as Collation, or reading before the evening service of Compline. These are the remains of a canopied seat in the centre of the church wall, where the abbot sat whilst supervising Collation.

The remains of the collation seat in the cloister alley (south) next to the church.

Opposite this seat, a rectangular slight depression can be seen extending into the turf of the cloister garth. This probably represents a projecting bay for the Collation lectern, or reading desk, and no doubt allowed more light for the reader.

In the east cloister walk, in the wall of the north transept, are the remains of two round-headed cupboards. These were for storing the books used in the cloister, and date back as far as the twelfth century. The northern cupboard was blocked in the fifteenth century when the rebuilding of the cloister with a stone vaulted roof was begun. As suggested earlier, the scanty survival of this late work seems to indicate that little progress had been made before the Dissolution.

Right: *A twelfth-century book cupboard in the east cloister walk. To the left, the round head of a second cupboard is seen blocked by fifteenth-century alterations to the cloister (see also p.25).*

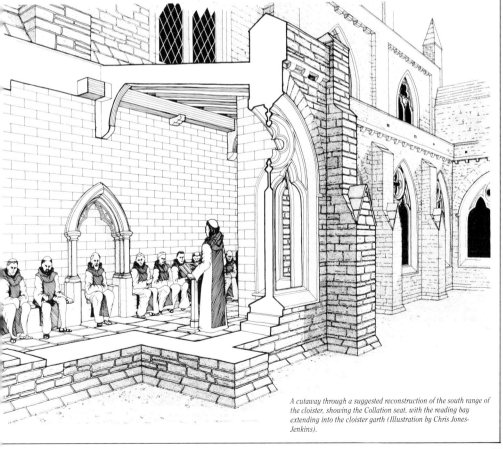

A cutaway through a suggested reconstruction of the south range of the cloister, showing the Collation seat, with the reading bay extending into the cloister garth (Illustration by Chris Jones-Jenkins).

The East Range

The eastern range in a Cistercian house was largely the domain of the choir monks. It is sometimes called the dormitory range since the first floor was occupied by the monks' sleeping quarters. At Tintern the east range measured some 170 feet (52m) from north to south. We may begin our tour at the southern end.

A general view looking down along the eastern range of the cloister. The chapter house is in the foreground, with the novices' lodging running into the distance. Above these, the full length of the first floor was occupied by the monks' dormitory.

Book Room and Sacristy

Adjoining the north transept, a finely carved fourteenth-century doorway, with a central mullion, leads into a long room, originally divided into two by a solid wall. The front part was used as the book room, where the abbey library was kept.

The elaborate fourteenth-century doorway into the book room.

The rear part could only be entered from the church and served as the sacristy. Part of the vaulted roof survives in this room, and there is a locker in the south wall. Above the sacristy a doorway led from the monks' dormitory to the abbey treasury, the place where all precious ornaments were stored.

The Chapter House

The next chamber to the north was the chapter house, second only to the church in importance. It was the administrative and disciplinary centre of the abbey, where the monks met each day with the abbot to commemorate saints, to hear a chapter of the Rule of St Benedict (from which the room took its name), to correct faults, and to transact the business of the house.

The bases of clustered pillars show that the entrance, of three equal openings, would have been richly carved. The delicate rib-vaulted roof was supported on the eight pillars partially surviving inside, and originally dividing the room into three bays across its width. It was lit by a large window in the east end, and by side windows in the farthest bay from the entrance, the southern one having to be blocked when the sacristy was completed.

A fifteenth-century illustration of St Bernard (d.1153) preaching in the chapter house at Clairvaux Abbey, showing how such a room was used. Such a scene was no doubt common at Tintern. From Jean Fouquet's Livre d'Heures d'Étienne Chevalier (By courtesy of Musée Condé, Chantilly; photograph by Giraudon).

Remains of the richly clustered shafts around the doorways into the chapter house (Illustration by Delyth Lloyd).

The monks sat on a stone bench which ran round the sides of the room. In most Cistercian monasteries it was customary to bury the deceased abbots in the chapter house. Although we have no positive evidence of the practice at Tintern, the five grave slabs in the cloister walk opposite the door perhaps came from within the chamber. Further decorative grave slabs, visible on old prints, are known from elsewhere in this walk.

A print of about 1850, showing a large double grave slab below the processional doorway in the east range of the cloister. The slab, which includes an inscription to Henry Lancaut, an abbot of Tintern's Irish daughter house, now lies in the sacristy.

Parlour

The room north of the chapter house was the parlour, where necessary conversation could be conducted without breaking the silence and study of the cloister. It was lit by a narrow window in the east side, and had an elaborate doorway from the cloister.

The small space north of the parlour probably contained the original day stairs to the monks' dormitory, but no traces remain. North of this once more is a passage which led from the cloister to the infirmary buildings.

The Novices' Lodging

The remainder of the eastern range at Tintern was probably given over to the novices. These were new entrants to the monastery, who underwent a period of probation before graduating as monks.

When completed in the thirteenth century, this was a fine hall, with a stone-vaulted roof supported on central pillars. The bases of these survive, as well as several of the contemporary narrow lancet windows in the side walls. When the vault was inserted, buttresses were added to the outside for additional support.

One of the narrow lancet windows inserted into the novices' lodging in the early thirteenth century (Illustration by Delyth Lloyd).

Towards the northern end of this room, it is possible to observe certain details of the main abbey drain. At this point, within the now open drain, sharply grooved stones at each side mark the position of sluice gates. The water level would have been raised before it was released through to the monks latrine (p.43). Raising the water level also released water through a higher, secondary, channel running north-east towards the abbots complex (pp.50-1).

The novices' lodging, which survives as part of the twelfth-century east range. The central pillars were added in the early thirteenth century to support a stone vault.

The Monks' Dormitory

The monks' dormitory occupied the entire first floor of the eastern range, but few of its details survive. Looking south from the novices' lodging we see the pitch of its roof revealed against the transept of the church. The range was laid out centrally with the transepts of the original church, but is overlapped by the wider transepts of the later building.

The foundations of the monks' latrine, with the channel of the abbey drain running through to the right (north).

The pitch of the monks' dormitory roof seen against the north transept of the church. Notice that the transept window (p.37) could not be carried below this roof level (Illustration by John Banbury).

At the southern end, above the sacristy, was the abbey treasury. The sacrist, who was in charge of this had his bed in this area. The remaining beds were laid out in dormitory fashion, though in the later Middle Ages demands for greater privacy often led to the insertion of wooden partitions.

The monks left their dormitory to attend services by either of two routes. Night-time services were approached directly through the north transept via the night stairs. In daylight hours, however, they used the day stairs in a passage to the east of the northern range. From here they walked through the cloister, and entered the church via the processional door.

The Latrine

Projecting from the north-east side of this range was the latrine block. There would have been direct access to this from the dormitory. The block was divided by a wall, and to the south it was vaulted with a door and windows facing the infirmary cloister. The northern half contained the drain, and above it was situated a row of cubicles, possibly at ground and first-floor level.

Retracing our steps back through the passage at the southern end of the novices' lodging, we move on to the buildings of the northern range.

The North Range

The principal building in the northern range was the monks' dining hall, with a kitchen to the west and warming house to the east. The arrangement we see today dates from the early thirteenth century, and the eastern part still stands to second-floor level.

The north range of the cloister from the south-east. This range was largely rebuilt in the early thirteenth century (see also pp.18-19).

Beginning at the east, the archway from the cloister leads to a narrow vaulted passage, with two more arches at its northern end. The smaller arch, to the west, contains a doorway leading out into an open yard. That to the east led to the day stairs into the dormitory. Walking through to the north and turning about, one will notice the higher level of this arch, allowing headroom on the stairs.

The taller arch, out from the rear of the north range, led to the day stairs into the monks' dormitory (to the left). The smaller arch gave access to an open yard.

Top: *A suggested reconstruction of the warming house, the only place where a fire was permitted in the abbey, apart from the infirmary and kitchens (Illustration by Chris Jones-Jenkins).*

Above: *The warming house, with its vault surviving in the southern half of the room. The northern end is reduced to foundation level.*

Warming House

The first chamber to the west is the warming house. Its name describes its purpose, for in the early Middle Ages, it was the only room in the monastery, except for the kitchens and infirmary, where a fire was kept burning in the winter months. The Cistercians also used it for the periodical bleeding of the brethren for reasons of health.

There was a central fireplace supported on four square pillars. The arched passageways on either side gave all-round access to the fire, so the monks could restore circulation to their chilled limbs after hours spent in the cold of the cloister and church. On the north, part of the hooded cowl of the fireplace is still in position. Further north, the room extended beyond the upper floors, and had a projecting gabled roof whose line can be readily seen. In later centuries the central fireplace went out of use, the chimney was blocked, and a new smaller fireplace built at the north end of the room.

The upper floors are no longer accessible, but the first storey comprised two rooms with small windows to the north and south. These rooms were reached from the dormitory, and they apparently served as an apartment for the prior. It was his duty to see good order kept in the dormitory itself. In the early sixteenth century a second storey was added, and characteristically

Tudor windows can be identified on the northern side. The chamber here perhaps provided lodgings for a senior monk, or even a corrodian at the house.

The Monks' Dining Hall

At the centre of the north cloister walk, a large doorway opens into the monks' dining hall. On either side of this once grand entrance are two arched recesses, and in each case the larger one contained a trough or, bowls where the monks washed before meals, with the smaller one holding towels.

Inside, it is a large room measuring 84 by 29 feet (26 x 9m). On the east side, the four-light windows, set in pairs, with their heavy plate tracery, give a reasonable impression of the

original appearance. In the centre of the west wall a doorway gave access to a slight projection which housed a pulpit. Here one of the monks stood during meals, and read to his brothers from the

Above: The monks' dining hall as it appears today, with the doorway into the pulpit seen to the left.

Below: A suggested impression of the monks' dining hall looking north. The high table is situated at the far end, and a monk reads to his brothers from the pulpit (Illustration by Chris Jones-Jenkins).

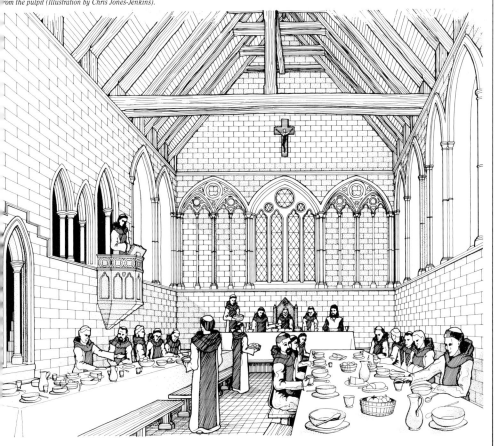

Bible. The roof was probably supported upon timber trusses set between each pair of windows and dividing the hall into four bays.

The prior presided over meals, and sat on a high table across the northern end. The monks sat on tables along the length of the hall and during early centuries were allowed to eat bread, cheese, eggs, fish, fruit or potage, but not meat.

In the south-east corner of the hall a door leads to a small vaulted pantry or storeroom. Close by, in the south wall, are two recesses. That on the left with a drain was for washing plates and spoons, and the other was for storing them.

The south-east corner of the dining hall, with a doorway leading into the pantry, and two small recesses where dishes were washed and stored after meals (Illustration by John Banbury).

At the other side of the entrance, in the south end of the west wall, there is a serving hatch from the kitchen, not unlike a modern dining room arrangement. Finally, in the end wall nearby is a recess intended for a drop-down table.

Kitchen

The remainder of the north range was taken up with the kitchen. It was placed where it could serve both the choir monks and the lay brothers. Unfortunately, the internal layout was much destroyed by a post-medieval cottage on the site.

It seems that a wall running north to south (see plan) divided the building in two. The eastern part, with a doorway to the cloister, was used as the servery. To the north of this, in a slight extension, was perhaps a scullery. The larger room to the west had doorways to the cloister, the west range and to a yard on the north. Wood is likely to have been stored in this yard and carried through to the great fire positioned in the dividing wall.

The West Range

As with other Cistercian houses, during the early Middle Ages, the buildings on the western side of the cloister were almost entirely occupied by the lay brethren. The total length of the range at Tintern was at least 180 feet (55m). We may begin our tour at the northern end.

The Lay Brothers' Dining Hall and Dormitory

A skew-passage in the north-west corner of the cloister leads into a long and relatively narrow chamber. Few details have survived, but it was originally a vaulted room, and the lower part of the ground area served as the lay brothers' dining hall. Access from the kitchen was through a doorway on the south-east side. Part of this ground floor may, as at Neath, have been a common room for the labouring monks.

The abbey drain crosses below the hall, and just to the north of this are the slight remains of a twelfth-century doorway. It must have belonged to the early layout of buildings and was presumably discarded when the existing range was constructed.

Skew-passage into the west range from the cloister. The lay brothers' dining hall was on the ground floor, with their dormitory above.

There have been suggestions that the northern end of the range may have extended further, and perhaps housed the lay brothers' infirmary as in a contemporary structure at Beaulieu Abbey. But there is no reason to suppose this was not a separate building, somewhere to the west under the modern car park, in a similar place to one at the sister abbey of Waverley. The lay brothers' latrine must also have been somewhere in that area.

The entire upper floor was occupied by the dormitory of the lay brethren. However, as in the nave of the church, with the decline of this brotherhood in the fourteenth century, alternative uses were surely found for both floors. We can only guess at these, though examples of private apartments, storage and even agricultural uses are all known from other Cistercian houses.

Cellar

To the south of the lay brothers' accommodation is a square vaulted chamber with no direct opening to the cloister. It had a doorway to the north and another to the west, and appears to have been used as a cellar.

Porch and Outer Parlour

Projecting from the south-western end of this range, and approached from the west door of the cellar, is a late thirteenth-century porch through which medieval visitors might enter the inner

parts of the monastery. It has a stone bench on its south side and a large arched recess on the north. Through the porch we enter the outer parlour, where the monks could meet and converse with tradesmen and other visitors. Both these rooms eventually had vaulted ceilings.

In the north-west corner of the outer parlour a small doorway gave access to a stair leading to the two rooms above, and these formed the cellarer's lodging. From here he could not only oversee good order among the lay brothers, but also represent the house on business and estate matters when visitors arrived below.

In the south wall of the parlour a large door opened on to a covered walk by which the lay brothers reached the abbey church. On the east side of the walk are the remains of the stairway which led, by way of a passage, down from their dormitory to the entrance in the north-west corner of the church. Looking north towards the southern wall of the cellarer's lodging, notice the remains of a thirteenth-century window with one of the following century inserted. The small court

The lay brothers' cloister, with the stairs down from their dormitory in the far corner. To the right is their doorway into the nave of the abbey church.

The porch and outer parlour at the southern end of the west range. The upper floor of the parlour, now roofless, was probably occupied by the abbey's cellarer (Illustration by John Banbury).

in this area probably served as a cloister for the lay brethren, and at the north of its east wall are the remains of a square tank for storage of water.

From this point, the visitor may care to continue the tour by passing back through the main cloister and out via the passage in its north-east corner. This leads to a smaller cloister and, beyond this, the infirmary complex.

The Infirmary

The infirmary housed both the sick and aged monks, and for this reason tended to lie in the most secluded part of a medieval monastery. Although Tintern must have had an infirmary in the twelfth century, this was probably of wood, and, as with Cistercian houses in general, was replaced in stone in the thirteenth century. The centre of the complex was the great hall.

Infirmary Hall

Unfortunately, the large hall does not survive to any great height and so it is difficult for us to appreciate that in origin, after the church, it was probably the most attractive building in the abbey. When built, it appeared almost as a church, with a central nave, an aisle at either side, and measured some 107 by 54 feet (33 x 16m).

The large infirmary hall from the south-west. To the left (north) are the infirmary kitchens, where more delicate and nourishing food was prepared.

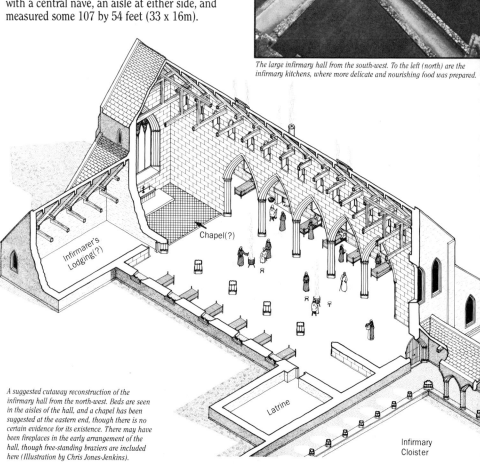

Infirmarer's Lodging(?)

Chapel(?)

Latrine

Infirmary Cloister

A suggested cutaway reconstruction of the infirmary hall from the north-west. Beds are seen in the aisles of the hall, and a chapel has been suggested at the eastern end, though there is no certain evidence for its existence. There may have been fireplaces in the early arrangement of the hall, though free-standing braziers are included here (Illustration by Chris Jones-Jenkins).

An elaborately carved doorway from the infirmary cloister was added in the fourteenth century. Inside, the north and south aisles were originally separated from the central nave by round pillars. The first bay at either end of each, however, was walled off from the outset. The bays within these aisles were lit by sets of paired lancet windows, whereas from excavations we know the great east wall was pierced by a much larger window filled with delicate stone tracery.

The room extending off the north-west corner has a drain at its northern end. This seems to have been the infirmary latrine. The large chamber on the north-east corner is more difficult to explain, but might have served as the infirmarer's lodging.

The beds were arranged in either aisle, and here the monks were cared for when the daily life in the cloister had become too severe. They were given more delicate and nourishing food than the normal monastic diet.

In the fifteenth century the aisles were separated from the central nave by screen walls. Demands for greater privacy led to the creation of 'private wards' within each. These were provided with a fireplace, with small cupboards or lockers to one side.

A fireplace and cupboard (right) inserted into the infirmary as part of the fifteenth-century alterations. 'Private wards' were virtually created, with a similar arrangement in each.

Sometimes infirmaries were provided with their own chapel, but there is no trace of this at Tintern. A passage, formerly covered, leads directly from the infirmary hall to the abbey church.

Infirmary Kitchen

A doorway in the north of the hall leads to the infirmary kitchen. This was built in the early fifteenth century, and enlarged soon after, but must have replaced an earlier structure. The initial building is to the west, with a fireplace in the east wall. The massive lintel rests broken in two in front of the hearth. A passage to the south

A large lintel resting in front of one of the fireplaces in the infirmary kitchens.

gave access to the later extension, which had great fireplaces in both the east and west walls. The door at the south opened towards the infirmary hall, and on the north the smaller room was a scullery. To the north-east are the foundations of a fourteenth-century building which must have been destroyed when the later kitchen was built.

These new kitchens were probably built not only in response to demands for higher standards in the infirmary, but also to serve the corrodians and retired senior monks who had taken up residence in various rooms in this part of the monastery.

Infirmary Cloister

The gradual development of these infirmary buildings gave rise to an open court or second cloister. This measures some 84 by 71 feet (26 x 22m), and was possibly a place of relaxation for the infirmary inmates.

The Abbot's Accommodation

The remaining buildings to the north-east of the infirmary cloister can all be considered under the heading of accommodation for the abbot. As stated, the early Cistercian custom whereby abbots were required to sleep in the common dormitory with the monks was soon overlooked. At Tintern, the abbot first appears to have acquired separate quarters in the early thirteenth century (p.20).

Early Buildings

To begin with, the abbot was probably housed in the block situated to the east of the monks' latrine, on the north side of the later infirmary cloister. The ground floor was divided into two rooms, the larger of which had a doorway to the south and a window in the north end of its east wall. The upper storey was almost certainly linked to the latrine itself, thereby keeping the abbot technically under the same roof as the dormitory.

By the fourteenth century a fireplace had been inserted in the western of the ground-floor rooms. The entire block had been given over to corrodians, or else it formed some other kind of private apartments.

This room, with that where the figure stands beyond, was probably the ground floor of the early abbot's lodging. By the later Middle Ages it may have been turned over to private apartments.

The other well-preserved two-storey block to the north-east was also constructed in the early thirteenth century. As suggested, it may have been intended as a visiting abbot's house (p.20), but was soon taken over by the abbot of Tintern himself. The upper floor provided a living room, with a subvaulted chamber below.

The Later Hall

The growing status and importance of the abbot are reflected in an extensive rebuilding at his quarters during the fourteenth century. By this time his rôle had come to appear little different from that of any secular landed magnate. Consequently, not only did he feel justified in

The early abbot's house in the foreground, with the lower levels of the late medieval, and much larger hall to the rear. To the top right are the remains of the abbot's later private apartments.

accepting a certain degree of style and comfort, it was also a matter of pure necessity in order to entertain and accommodate illustrious guests and benefactors.

The most notable addition was a new hall, built on a grand scale. Unfortunately, only the storerooms or cellars of the lower floor can be identified. But even so, these lower levels with their high-quality stonework around the numerous doors, and fine corner buttresses, all

splay confidence with little consideration for
st. The great hall, no doubt with an elaborate
mber roof, stood on the upper floor.

Other additions at the time included a chapel
ock to the south of the abbot's house. The
hapel had a two-light east window, and the
emains of a piscina survive in the south wall. A
trine was constructed to the east, and adjacent
o this a dovecot, common on later medieval
manorial sites, but all traces of this have now
disappeared.

The Abbey Precinct

This completes our tour of the major surviving
buildings at Tintern Abbey. We should
appreciate, however, that these did not stand in
isolation. The abbey church and domestic
structures were situated within a large walled
precinct covering some 27 acres (11ha). Indeed,
his was larger than the area enclosed by the walls
f several medieval towns in south-east Wales.

Remains of the precinct wall can be seen to the
west, and to the south of the modern road. The
wall was entered through a gatehouse on the
south-west side and close to this was the
gatehouse chapel which still survives as part of a
private house. To the west of the modern entrance
to the abbey, close to the inn, are the remains of a
second gateway which led to the slipway for the
ferry across the Wye.

Outer Court

A considerable area of the abbey's precinct was
taken up with the outer court, which lay in the
flat area to the west of the abbey church. This was
the place which contained all the other buildings
necessary for the efficient running of a monastery.

Various ruins can be seen in this area at
Tintern, and recent excavations have revealed
details of a guest-house, as well as evidence of late
medieval industrial activity. But the outer court
would also have included the abbey mill, stables, a
bakehouse, perhaps even a secular infirmary,
together with a host of other structures vital to
the economic side of monastic life.

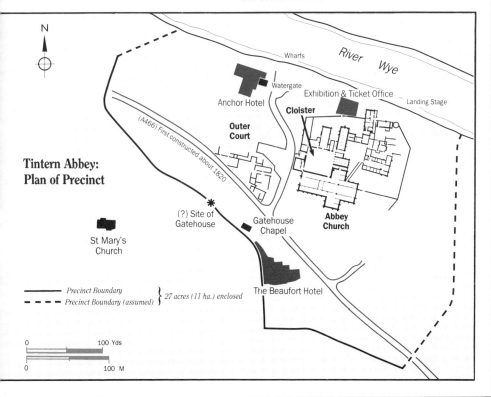

Tintern Abbey:
Plan of Precinct

IV Resurrection:
Tourists Discover Tintern

In the centuries after the Dissolution of the Monasteries, the demand for building stone meant that they were often systematically robbed for new building in the vicinity. As a result, the remains of once large and famous abbeys have now all but vanished. Happily, the absence of any town or large village close to Tintern seems to have preserved its ruins from total despoliation in this way. Nonetheless, the post-Dissolution centuries were to witness significant changes in this part of the Wye valley.

A watercolour of the crossing within the abbey church, by J.M.W. Turner (1775-1851). At the time of Turner's visits to the Wye valley in the 1790s, Tintern was at the height of its 'romantic' appeal (By courtesy of the Ashmolean Museum, Oxford).

Iron mills in the Angidy valley, near Tintern Abbey, from an engraving published in 1798.

Ironworking at Tintern

From the sixteenth century onwards, Tintern was to become important for its industrial activity, and for the manufacture of iron wire. Metalworking already had something of a history here. Recent archaeological excavations, west of the abbey church, show that copper and lead smelting began through monastic enterprise in later medieval times. The wireworks established in 1566 was, however, something quite new, both in raw materials, scope and scale. The attraction for this early industry was an ample supply of water power in the Angidy valley west of the former abbey. Over the next 200 years the whole area was developed with a series of small ironworks, forges and associated industrial processes.

Some of this industry was to encroach upon the monastic precinct since the level ground around the abbey must have remained at a premium. Numerous cottages were built in and around the ruins, but the stone robbed for these perhaps came from the domestic buildings around the cloister, rather than from the church.

The Romantic Movement

For two centuries after the departure of the monks, whilst industry had begun to flourish in the adjacent Angidy valley, few would have bothered to travel to view the ruins of Tintern Abbey. In the sixteenth and seventeenth centuries wild scenery, like that of the Wye valley, was regarded with dislike rather than affection. This was also reflected in fashionable homes of the day, with their neat formal gardens. Moreover, the regard for classical architecture made the medieval gothic style seem ugly, even barbarous.

In 1732, the Buck brothers published the first
ingraving of Tintern, and recorded the abbey
much as we see it today. Gradually, as the century
progressed, interest in gothic buildings began to
e-emerge. Such new interest may explain the
luke of Beaufort's efforts to curb some of the
neglect at Tintern. In 1756 the church was
cleared of debris, and the ground levelled and
turfed. The thick screen of ivy, which by then
covered most of the walls, was to remain as part of
the attraction of the ruins. In fact, it would be
lifficult to explain the duke's action in terms of
conservation', or even a search for antiquarian
knowledge. On the contrary, Tintern, like scores of
other ruined medieval abbeys and castles, was
becoming the focus for sentimental and romantic
study. Throughout the country, travellers were
finding a fearful joy, an awe, in 'surrendering to
the sublime effect' of such ruins.

The French Revolution (1789-99) indirectly
gave an impetus to the movement which
rediscovered the beauties of the wild landscapes of
Great Britain, and also to the 'Romantic
Movement' which accompanied it. The Revolution
made travel abroad difficult, and soon the wild
scenery of the Wye valley was to become a
substitute for that of Switzerland or the Rhine.
Tintern, with its 'romantic' and beautiful
countryside, was to attract a growing number of
visitors.

In the closing years of the eighteenth century,
tourists were sailing down the Wye from Ross to
Chepstow in boats laden with comforts and picnic
hampers. Many of these early tourists are likely to
have carried a copy of William Gilpin's best-selling
handbook, *Observations on the River Wye ...*
(London 1782), which offered them principles by
which they might judge the 'correctness' and
'beauty' of a view. Gilpin was somewhat critical of
Tintern, and felt there was scope for making the
ruins more picturesque:

'Though the parts are beautiful, the
whole is ill-shaped ... a number of gable-
ends hurt the eye with their regularity;
and disgust it by the vulgarity of their
shape. A mallet judiciously used (but who
durst use it?) might be of service in
fracturing some of them...'

These considerations were not, however, to
deter the young artist J.M.W. Turner, who visited
the ruins on several occasions between 1792-98.
He was travelling extensively at the time, visiting
similar sites all over England and Wales, and
filling his sketch-books with numerous pencil
drawings. These provided the raw material for
finished watercolours, and a selection of superb
Tintern examples survives in public and private
collections.

Perhaps the most famous of these 'romantic'
visitors to Tintern was the poet, William
Wordsworth, who first visited the Wye Valley, as a
young man of 23, in 1793. He returned five years

even making moonlit visits, viewing every part by burning torchlight. Indeed, an indication of the growing number of early nineteenth century visitors is given by Charles Heath's *Descriptive Account of Tintern Abbey, Monmouthshire* (Monmouth 1793), which had passed into no less than its eleventh edition by 1828.

Visitors Continue to Arrive

The 'romantic' appeal of Tintern extended well into the Victorian period. Some, like W.H. Thomas in 1839, were disappointed at seeing the abbey 'encumbered on every side with unpicturesque cottages and pigsties, rudely built with the consecrated stones of the violated ruin'. But even opinions such as this were usually overcome by the 'indescribable grandeur and beauty' of the interior.

The early Victorians were also confounded by the presence of screen walls dividing the church. To them, their relevance to Cistercian ritual was lost, and they were merely seen as destroying an otherwise superb vista. In particular, the *pulpitum*

later in the summer of 1798, and after several day's walking he wrote his *'Lines Composed a Few Miles above Tintern Abbey'*. He said of this work that 'No poem of mine was composed under circumstances more pleasant for me to remember than this'.

By 1800, the abbey ruins were that busy tourist attraction which was to greet William Coxe. So popular had the site become, that tourists were

Tourists exploring the interior of the abbey church, from a lithograph published about 1850 (By courtesy of the National Library of Wales).

p.32–3) was felt to break that view from the east
o|the west ends of the church. Although it was
apparently still in position until 1854, it was later
removed on grounds of 'improvement'.

The Victorian period was also to see the
introduction of photography as a new medium for
recording 'romantic' views of the abbey, and it is
from such a photograph that we have some
indication as to the appearance of the now-lost
pulpitum. It was, however, rarely the detail which
appealed to the early photographers; like the
artists before them, it was the ivy-mantled whole
which they held so dear.

Towards the close of the nineteenth century,
there was a shift towards a scientific approach in
enquiring into the origins and development of
buildings such as Tintern. All over the country,
excavations and clearance, generally aimed at
recovering the plan of medieval structures, were
being undertaken. Soon after the turn of the
century the outline of the early stone church at
Tintern was recovered by the archaeologist's
spade under the direction of Sir Harold Brakspear.

In 1901 the site was bought by the Crown from
the duke of Beaufort. In 1914 it was transferred to
the then Office of Works, the predecessors of
Cadw: Welsh Historic Monuments.

The Office of Works quickly set about saving
the piers of the south nave arcade from collapse,

Consolidation work in progress on the south side of the abbey church in 1914.

and a new roof was placed over the south aisle
itself. The ivy, so beloved by the early tourists, but
which caused much decay in the stonework, was
removed. Gradually, post-medieval encroachments
were cleared away, and more of the original
buildings uncovered and displayed. Most recently,
excavations in the outer court area, west of the
church, have exposed remains which will

eventually be consolidated and add to our
understanding of the monastic life at Tintern.

The number of visitors has continued to rise
over the last half-century. The beauty is timeless
and, standing amid the peaceful ruins, one can
perhaps still sense the spirit which drew that very
first community of monks to Tintern over 850
years ago.

Further Reading

This guide has passed through several
previous and informative editions since
Tintern Abbey was first taken into the care of the
State in 1901. Earlier versions were produced on
behalf of HM Office of Works, later the Ministry
of Public Building and Works and later still the
Ancient Monuments Branch of the Welsh Office.
In particular, the present text owes much to the
former 'blue' guides:

Sir Harold Brakspear,*Tintern Abbey
Monmouthshire* (HMSO, London 1934).
O.E. Craster, *Tintern Abbey Monmouthshire*
(HMSO, London 1956).

Further background on the Cistercians in Wales
and specific details on the history of Tintern
have been taken from:

F.G. Cowley, *The Monastic Order in South Wales
1066-1349* (Cardiff 1977).
J.M. Lewis and D.H. Williams, *The White Monks
in Wales* (Cardiff 1976) — the catalogue of an
exhibition staged in the National Museum of
Wales.
D.H. Williams, *White Monks in Gwent and the
Border* (Pontypool 1976) — especially pp. 94-146
which are devoted to Tintern.
D.H. Williams, *The Welsh Cistercians*, 2nd ed, 2
vols (Caldey Island 1984).

Other works of related interest, and where
further references can be found, include:

R.A. Donkin, *The Cistercians: Studies in the
Geography of Medieval England and Wales*
(Toronto 1978).
R. Gilyard-Beer, *Abbeys: An Illustrative Guide to
the Abbeys of England and Wales*, 2nd ed (HMSO,
London 1976).
J.K. Knight, *Tintern and the Romantic Movement*
(London 1977).
C.P.S. Platt, *The Abbeys and Priories of Medieval
England* (London 1984).

Abaty Tyndyrn — Crynodeb

Tŷ mynachod Sistersaidd yw Abaty Tyndyrn, a sefydlwyd gan Walter de Clare, Arglwydd Casgwent, ym 1131. Urdd fynachaidd yn hannu'n wreiddiol o Citeaux yn Burgundy yw'r Sistersiaid ac ym 1128 y gwelwyd hwy gyntaf ym Mhrydain. Fel eu tai eraill i gyd sefydlwyd Tyndyrn mewn mangre bellennig.

Dim ond seiliau'r adeiladau o'r ddeuddegfed ganrif a saif er y gellir gweld amlinell o'r hen eglwys yn llawer yr eglwys bresennol. Tua 1220, dechreuwyd ailadeiladu'r Abaty'n llwyr, ac felly y cafwyd yr adeiladau a welir heddiw. Ailadeiladwyd y gwahanol adeiladau o gwmpas y clas i ddechrau, ac ym 1270 dechreuwyd gweithio ar Eglwys newydd, yn rhannol ar draul Iarll Roger Bigod III o Gasgwent. Fe'i gorffennwyd ym 1301. Yn ystod diwedd yr Oesoedd Canol ni wnaed ond newid adeilad yr Abad a'r ysbyty.

Ym 1536 diddymwyd yr Abaty, a'r flwyddyn ganlynol rhoddwyd y safle i Henry, Iarll Caerwrangon. Yng nghyfnod Elizabeth, adeiladwyd gweithfeydd gwifrau yn Nghyndyrn, ac yn ddiweddarach adeiladwyd bythynnod yn yr Abaty ac o'i gwmpas. Yn 1901, prynwyd y safle oddi wrth Ddug Beaufort gan y Goron.

Mae'r Eglwys wedi parhau fwy neu lai yn gyfan, ac eithrio ffordd gysgodol y corff gogleddol, a oedd wedi diflannu erbyn 1801. Safai'r Allor Uchel ychydig i'r gorllewin o'r pâr cyntaf o birau. Y tu ôl iddo gwelir o hyd rwyllwaith y ffenestr ddwyreiniol ond y mae'r gwydr herodraidd a gariai arfbais y sefydlydd ar goll. Dros y groesfan, sydd wedi cadw'i phedwar bwa, ceid clochdy isel. Roedd Côr y Mynachod o dan y groesfan, a rhennid rhan ddwyreiniol y corff oddi wrth y corff ei hun — a ddefnyddid gan y brodyr lleyg a'r ymwelwyr — gan sgrîn gain o garreg, neu *pulpitum*. Yn y Croesau ac yn erbyn Mur Dwyreiniol yr Eglwys, ceid cyfres o wyth allor, er mwyn i'r mynachod gael dweud yr offeren bob dydd. Goroesodd rhai cerrig bedd o'r oesoedd canol ynghyd â malurion o fwâu.

Yn y clas, y gyfres nesaf at yr Eglwys oedd yr un a gedwid yn draddodiadol ar gyfer myfyrio, a gellir gweld sedd y Prior a arferai gadw trefn yno. Yn y gyfres Ddwyreiniol ceir yr Ystafell Lyfrau a'r Festri; y Cabildyldy lle'r ymgasglai'r mynachod bob dydd, ynghyd â pharlwr. Mae'r Gyfres Ogleddol yn cynnwys yr ystafell gynhesu neu'r ystafell gyffredin, yr Ystafell Fwyta, a'r gegin. Yn y Gyfres Orllewinol y trigai'r Brodyr Lleyg, a

defnyddid hon i storio hefyd. I'r dwyrain o'r clasai ceid dau grŵp o adeiladau lle trigai'r Abad a'i weision, a'r mynachod oedd yn hen ac yn fethedig I ddechrau neuadd oedd yr olaf, sef yr Ysbyty, onc wedyn fe'i trowyd yn gyfres o ystafelloedd unigol gyda lleoedd tân.

Cynhwysid 27 erw i gyd o fewn muriau'r fynachlog a gellir gweld rhan o'r mur cylchynnol hyd. I'r Gorllewin o'r Abaty gwelir olion adeiladau sy'n cael eu clirio ar hyn o bryd, yn cynnwys y gwesty, a thros y ffordd gwelir capel tŷ porth bychan St Anne.

Tour of the Abbey — A Summary

The numbers on the plan, opposite, are intended to help the visitor follow the principal features covered in the guided route in the above text. Page numbers are given in brackets.

1 *The west front (p.26)*
2 *The nave; lay brothers' church (pp.32-3)*
3 *North and south aisles (p.33)*
4 *The monk's choir and the crossing (pp.34-5)*
5 *The presbytery (p.35)*
6 *South transept (p.36)*
7 *North transept (p.37)*
8 *The Cloister (pp.38-9)*
9 *Chapter house (pp.40-1)*
10 *Novices' lodging; monks dormitory above (pp.42-3)*
11 *Warming house (p.44)*
12 *Dining hall (pp.45-6)*
13 *Lay brothers' range (pp.46-7)*
14 *Infirmary complex (pp.48-9)*
15 *The abbot's accommodation (pp.50-1)*